MASTERING CONFRONTATION

Become an Expert at Effective Communication. Master the Art of Dealing with Conflict

Robert Hunt

professional before attempting any techniques outlined in this book.

By reading this document, the reader agrees that under no circumstances is the author responsible for any losses, direct or indirect, that are incurred as a result of the use of the information contained within this document, including, but not limited to, errors, omissions, or inaccuracies.

Table of Contents

Introduction

Conflict - a one-word recipe for disaster, stress and nervous breakdown for many. A part of life that is dreaded, loathed yet remains unavoidable. Regardless of how well we try to handle matters, conflict finds its way to tamper with the moment and makes it difficult for us to manage.

We all face conflicts every day in our lives. Whether we try and go on a quick shopping trip with our significant others, decide on a location for our next trip, or try to propose a better way to move ahead with our latest products, we will cross paths with conflict every single time.

For something that is so unavoidable, it makes less sense to try and find a way to avoid such situations. However, it does make more sense to navigate through the problem with justified reasoning and a desirable solution. To do exactly that, I have gone through some of the trickiest situations and decided to jot down all the strategies which truly hold value and can teach us how to manage and deal with conflicting situations as they arise.

Some methods will test our tolerance while others will allow us to remain assertive instead of being aggressive; a common issue faced by many.

The book will bring forth various concepts and ideas which will be explained thoroughly, therefore you do not need to be an expert or have prior knowledge about psychology or conflict management. Any professional or adult should easily be able to relate, understand and take away some valuable tips and tricks from this book to apply when the time is right.

What Will You Get Out of This Book?

Quite a lot, to be honest. I have taken every possible method into consideration and decided to only list out, and explain, the ones which truly hold profound impacts and allow an individual to gain the upper hand in a conflicting situation.

This book aims to highlight, boost, teach and provide in-depth facts about:

- Communication - Unknown to many, clear communication is a vital component in conflict management.

- Intrapersonal skills - Highlight abilities within ourselves to identify errors, issues, and negativity.

- Productive ways to manage conflict - The central idea of the book.

- What is conflict? - Sure enough, to get to the root of the problem, you first need to learn about it.

- Accept mistakes

- Be a good listener

There are quite a few more which we will come across, but the above are the ones which we will often encounter. As I mentioned earlier, there will be moments where our tolerance will be tested. The last two points I mentioned above reflect in such situations. We will get into more detail later on.

The book further aims to provide you with various exercises and hence allow you to learn how to identify conflicts and learn how to manage them effectively and quickly.

"Knowing is half the battle!" - G.I. Joe

I have always found that to be a powerful quote from a fiction series of G.I. Joe. It is true that without knowledge, we will only fear everything. It is only through knowledge that we start understanding matters better and stop fearing things.

Through knowledge, we will learn how to stop fearing conflicts. There are many of us who cave in and give in to the fear of conflicts, often causing us to allow others to make important decisions for us, even if we do not like those. Through knowledge, we will learn how to control our instincts and apply logical reasoning to stand our ground and face even the toughest situations without fear, intimidation or worries.

The journey to conquer our fears starts with a single step. If you have decided you no longer wish to be caught in the heat of the situation and cave in every time a conflict arises, take a deep breath and take the first step forward. Let this book be your guide to conquer your insecurities and allow you to be more successful in life, both professional and otherwise.

Who Am I?

Naturally, one of the first things a person would inquire about would be the author. Is the author a credible person or even qualified enough to answer questions such as *how to handle conflicts at work without losing my temper?* or *how to prove I am right without offending the other party?*

My name is Robert Hunt. I am a psychologist with years of experience, knowledge, and practice. Apart from being a psychologist, I am also a life coach. Combined, I have well over 20 years of experience as a motivational speaker and a therapist.

Throughout my professional career, I have come across various instances, clients and patients who have struggled with a lot of things within life. Some of these were as simple as arguments erupting between a couple on a regular basis to something more concerning as shutting themselves out into isolation and letting others take control of their lives.

While I did get the knowledge I needed to practice, the true knowledge came in the form of cases, where each client presented a unique issue to deal with. It did not take me long to realize that most of the patients suffered either from stress or had no idea how to deal with conflicts. Both are natural, both are interconnected but both require special attention.

As a life coach and psychologist, I have worked with various entrepreneurs, professionals, and clients, and effectively helped them to be more confident and assertive instead of being aggressive or intimidated. I have also had the privilege of working with some leading firms as a business consultant to further tweak and fine-tune their corporate strategies.

As time passed, I shifted my attention and decided to focus more on the masses over a client or two. Now, I write books about stress management, conflict resolution, communication and ways to ensure lasting, positive changes in life. I aim to spread knowledge to the readers, specifically the ones who are looking to step out of the shadows and shine bright by being more confident, sharp and ready to face conflicts and resolve them.

As a young boy, I was a high school Football Captain. It did not take long for me to hold an additional charge of a coach for the junior teams. This additional duty served as the turning point in life.

Do you know the feeling that you need a spark to ignite your curiosity? I had just experienced that. This is the sole reason I pursued Psychology from NYU (1994), with the intention to understand how the human mind and body work and learn how to improve performance while reducing stress.

My wife happened to work in the ER, and one tragic day, she had an incident. She suffered from severe burnout. Just when I thought I knew how to cope with things, I realized I was helpless as I was unable to do anything but watch. I was unable to help my wife out in ways she needed me.

There are times where you feel completely lost, only to come to a point where you rediscover yourself. Sure, I would have hoped for better ways to meet a new turning point in my life, but then again, some things are just beyond our control. This tragic incident is what led me to seek a second degree, this time as a life coach.

I learned about alternative healing methods, impacts of lifestyle choices and so on. The more I learned, the more it became clear to me that things are far more than just psychological.

I started serving the people around me with all that I knew, and fortunately, it started to show promising results. One thing led to another and soon I started writing books. The path to discovery certainly took a few turns, but I am glad that my learning experiences can now be used to help others to learn and develop themselves into more confident and successful human beings.

Throughout the book, I will be sharing some of the most fascinating, thought-provoking, and astonishing ideas that I encourage everyone to try. Conflicts can happen even when you least expect them, and my aim is to provide you with all the tools and knowledge to prepare you to deal with any kind of conflict which may involve the most difficult of people.

It takes practice, and I will never claim that you can become a master at dealing with conflict within a day or two. Practice on your own, as much as you can. It takes time but the results are always worth the wait. With that said, let us get started on our journey and see how we can learn how to deal with conflicts more effectively.

Chapter 1:
Accepting Conflict as a Normal Part of Life

Talking about life, there are far too many things which are considered as normal whereas, in reality, they are anything but normal. Similarly, there are quite a few aspects of life which are considered odd or unusual, whereas they are absolutely common and normal. It is only how we perceive matters that makes a difference.

Conflict is a part of life that is neither unnatural nor avoidable. You can either use conflict and manage it constructively or you can cave in, in which case the results may very well be catastrophic in nature.

Our minds work in an odd fashion. The minute someone says stress or conflict, we immediately associate arguments or fights. Naturally, we are letting ourselves dwell in false concepts which further amplifies and fuels the issue at hand, making it tougher to manage than it actually should have been.

Quite a lot of research has actually gone into understanding what conflict is and how it can be dealt with, and the first thing that always seems to appear is the inability to accept conflict as a normal part of life. Almost everyone takes conflict as anything but normal. The heightened attention and different perception of conflict are what immediately make matters worse.

You cannot hope to derive results without first establishing a solid understanding of what conflict is and why should you not be afraid of it. To most of us, conflict is an argument or clash of opinions that can get quite ugly in nature. Half of that statement is true, while the other half is our perception that has been developed over time through exposure to something traumatic, hearing about other people arguing and bickering, portrayal in movies, social media and so on. It's time to put that nonsense to rest and focus on what conflict truly is.

Understanding Conflict Properly

Consider this as a basic lesson; without it, you will not be able to move forward. It is just like trying to build a skyscraper on a foundation that is hollow and weak. The building, regardless of its design, will eventually collapse. Build a solid foundation of concepts and then move forward to take a more productive approach towards resolving conflicts.

Conflict is defined as:

- A serious disagreement

- A clash of interests

- A dispute

- Difference of opinions

- Hostility

- A feud

- A war of words

- A disagreement characterized by hostility

All of these are indeed the definition of conflicts. Whether you have chosen one or two of these as your way of looking at conflict, it is your right to do so. However, even knowing what a conflict is, we still tend to add a perception to it.

Conflicts can generally arise anywhere. Most of us, owing to either traumatic past experiences or general misunderstandings, try and flee away from conflicts. These can easily unnerve us or make us lose our temper instantly.

Some of us try and seek conflict to test our own limits. We often end up creating a conflict deliberately, in hopes to see how the conflict arises and how we can cope with the issue. In either way, conflict is natural and needs to be resolved. Running away may not be the option you have every time, nor would caving in be feasible every time.

Conflict isn't something that erupts immediately either. There are factors which, if carefully observed, can highlight or indicate the imminent arrival of a conflict. For those who may be able to identify such signs, they may have just about enough time to sort issues out, hence ending the need for a conflict.

If conflict was to be divided into phases, there would generally be around five of them. Let us look at each one to further understand what leads to conflict, what happens while it remains and how it can end.

1. **Prelude to conflict** - This generally involves every type of factor that can lead to a conflict between groups, individuals, etc. These can include matters like lack of coordination, clash of thoughts, differences of opinions, educational or religious background and so on.

2. **Triggering Event** - It is understood that conflict needs a ground, a reason to start. Without one, a conflict would never arise. Whatever the factor or element that triggers a conflict to start falls under this phase. Imagine a presentation about cultures where a middle-eastern candidate is presenting ideas about his culture and

someone else from the west finds it absurd.

3. **Initiation Phase** - This is the phase where the conflict has just begun. Now, the arguments, the brawl, and war of words, heated debates, all of these would initiate the conflict and take it further.

4. **Differentiation Phase** - This is where everyone would be voicing their own opinions and differences against each other. Generally, this is the phase where the reasons for conflicts are raised.

5. **Resolution Phase** - Lastly, a conflict generally leads to nowhere. It is around this phase that individuals should realize and learn how to compromise to a certain extent to diffuse the situation and arrive at a resolution that is acceptable by both parties.

Here's a little exercise for you. Create a little list and jot down at least three conflicts which recently took place within the office or home, or even with friends. Try and identify the reasons.

For now, just a list of these conflicts would do. I will be asking you to use this list over and over again, with various iterations and changes to make learning a little more intuitive.

We have seen the phases, but what about the sources? Is it necessary that we always end up with conflict because someone else had to say something we did not quite accept? As it turns out, no!

There are various reasons which can lead to a conflict in the first place. The phases we discussed above matter only when a conflict is unavoidable. If you end up resolving the issue before the conflict arises, none of the above would ever take place. Therefore, let us look into some common sources of conflict which we should know about.

An American Psychologist named Daniel Katz proposed that there are three main sources that lead to conflict. These are:

1. **Economic conflict** - When resources are limited, individuals or groups of people can undergo a conflict to try and secure the most for themselves. These types of conflicts can normally be very hostile in nature.

2. **Value Conflict** - Mr. A has a different preference than Mrs. A. Similarly, Mr. B has a different set of ideologies than Mrs. B. In both cases, expect conflict to arise in an aggressive manner where each party

will try to assert their views and opinions over others.

3. **Power Conflicts** - This is generally seen with individuals or people who try to maximize their influence over society or a larger audience. These are generally seen in societies, communities and even on a global scale where politicians are always trying to control their narrative and influence.

I will not be wrong to say that conflict is a part of our experience, and quite a vital one as well. Learn how to deal with it, and you will come out as a successful person who is able to communicate effectively and retain his/her ground without undergoing arguments. Let it mount up and you allow yourself to burst one fine day.

An uncontrolled conflict can be extremely destructive. People have ended up causing physical harm and even gone to the extent of committing unethical and fatal crimes. Hundreds of thousands of murder cases took place owing to conflicts. Had these conflicts been managed more effectively, we would have seen a more peaceful world.

So, is conflict really that bad all the time? You may be surprised to hear this, but conflict can often do wonders for us. Sometimes, it is just the thing we need to spur ourselves back into action and regain the lost cause and motivation to do something productive.

A Positive Aspect!

Let me clarify one thing right away. A positive conflict does not suggest that the two parties arrived at a difference of opinion and laughed it out to resolve the issue. That is rarely the case.

Positive conflict is essentially a conflict that is constructive in nature. It is a conflict that drives a person to push the envelope further, blur the edges and think out of the box. This is the type of conflict that allows you to regain your composure, readjust your bearing and realign your center of focus.

Often, we come into a conflicting situation where we are arguing about something, and it is only then that we hit a moment of truth. We come across an epiphany that may very well serve the purpose, add value to our life or work while allowing us to be more effective and efficient at the same time. Think of the last argument you had at work where you realized you were looking at something from a different perspective and that you could easily change matters to never cause such issues again.

While I do not recommend the approach, I have still seen people making it a point of honor or set themselves with goals to prove critics wrong. This is only possible after you go through conflict; a positive one. Being met with criticism and harsh words often allows you to derive motivation from an otherwise dull situation. Now, you are more determined than ever before to prove your worth and prove to the critics how wrong they have been. Sounds relatable, right?

Throughout all the phases and types of conflicts, there is but one thing that remains constant: our ability to accept that conflict is natural. The sooner we accept that, the quicker we can move towards resolving the conflict or managing it accordingly.

The biggest hurdle that most of us face is the inability to accept conflict for what it is. We struggle with things like ego and prejudice, which only exacerbates the conflict. Our mind would normally perceive a conflict as a unique scenario; a scenario that should not have taken place and is not considered as ordinary. If you have been following the book so far, you would know by now that conflict is nothing but natural.

What is natural will always find its way into our lives. Dwell on that thought for a minute. Let it soak into your mind, that you cannot avoid conflict completely. You can only postpone it or speed it up by being a catalyst.

Begin by changing the way you think about conflicts. Not all conflicts need to end with heated debates and fistfights. You can take a more productive approach by looking at every conflict as an opportunity to present your best stance forward and learn how to be in control of the situation, without losing temper or control.

These are some of the defining character traits for any leader. If you can manage conflict productively and effectively, you can make quite an impression for yourself in any firm, surrounding or locality.

Changing our way of thinking and perspective can be quite a challenge. It is a lot easier for me to say this but when the same is tested in real life, it is truly an achievement. It is never easy to set aside our personal preferences, ego, and beliefs and start focusing on the fact that we actually might be wrong. Sometimes, you can immediately end a conflict just by admitting and realizing your mistake. As before, this is easier said than done.

Use conflicts to learn of your own mistakes and have the ability to identify your own flaws and accept them for what they are. Trying to defend yourself or your mistakes is only going to lead us away from the objective of this book. Our aim is to be more constructive and look at matters with a renewed purpose, intent and goal.

There are some emotional and cognitive traps that can catch most of us off-guard and further add to our worries. Try and see how these relate to you, and try to come up with a solution or a middle ground where both parties can hopefully reach an agreement.

Fairness Interpretations

This is perhaps the most common of the lot. We tend to look at things and rationalize what is right for us, instead of being more neutral and looking at the bigger picture. This approach is not only flawed but completely wrong. Our situation may differ from the other person and this is something we all need to understand. We try and force our views and justify what would be right by looking at aspects that relate to us.

Overconfidence

We, humans, are easily manipulated and can easily fall for traps and tricks without realizing the potential harm that awaits us at the end of the journey. Overconfidence is one such aspect. It is through our state of being overconfident about matters which leads us to set unrealistic expectations. Just because you may have hired a lawyer does not guarantee you a victory in a lawsuit. Needless to say, we still feel overconfident and it is through this simple factor that we may very well end up saying something that we may regret later on.

Commitment Escalation

Negotiators, who are often involved as mediators between parties trying to resolve a dispute or a conflict, tend to stick to their methods or course of action well after their usefulness. Trying to hold onto the same course of action, or sunken investments in a dispute such as time or legal fees, will only exacerbate matters and make things worse for us. These will play no role in the future and hence should be overlooked.

Conflict Avoidance

There are moments where we need a break. Some of us are able to get that much-needed break. But what about the ones who may not have the luxury of a quick getaway? Such individuals normally try and push these feelings down, in hopes that with time things will improve. The only thing such an action would do is to invite more trouble. Trying to avoid conflict will only delay matters and further add intensity.

All of the above are situations where conflict resolution is necessary. Without an effective resolution, the conflict will prevail and many would be left with severe stress and a bad day.

We already know the first step to resolve such issues; acceptance. By accepting conflict for what it is, analyzing the intensity and gravity of the situation, you are preparing yourself to take matters into your hands and steer all the parties away from further conflicting scenarios and into a more productive way of handling matters.

Let both the parties speak and let both be heard. There is a possibility they may arrive on mutually agreeable ground where both parties are happy with the resolution. There is also a possibility that one may understand their position is wrong, whereas the other would use the opportunity to further highlight the correct path. This is only made possible if both parties allow and accept conflict as a part of their lives. A constructive approach isn't enough on its own. If both the parties show a willingness to teach and to learn, conflicts of all types can be resolved far more effectively.

Look at conflicts as a general debate. Debates are often quite healthy and allow both sides to present their arguments and stances. In an ideal world, both parties will have an open mind to learn from the experience and be able to teach their views to the other party while showing respect and tolerance at the same time.

The chapters you will go through next will cover some of the most crucial aspects of conflict management and will play a vital role in diffusing a conflict peacefully and productively. Throughout the remaining chapters, we will see how the following help us in resolving conflicts:

- Talking to someone

- Exercising patience

- Focusing on the root of the problem

- Identifying where parties agree and disagree

- Prioritizing the aspects of conflict

- Planning to divert/diffuse the situation

All of that sounds good and effective, but all of them can only happen if you make your first move and become what is called an *Active Listener*. The next chapter will focus primarily on what active listening is and how we can use active listening to resolve a conflict. It is indeed a good idea to hear others out before you decide to take a course of action that may be completely unnecessary.

Chapter 2:
Become an Active Listener

Imagine sitting in a room where an important meeting is taking place. Sure, despite all your best efforts, there is still some background noise coming from the other side of the room. The meeting continues anyway and during the meeting, you rarely felt disturbed by the noise outside.

Here are a few questions for you to think about. Why were you able to understand everything within the meeting but not a single word that was spoken outside the room at the same time?

Now, turn this around and let us find ourselves in the same meeting room. This time, instead of focusing on the meeting itself, something interesting has caught our attention, and it is being discussed outside the room. During the meeting, we are trying to pay attention to the discussion outside while ensuring no one within this room feels annoyed or offended.

What do you think the result would be? Would you be able to hear the conversation outside and still be able to understand everything that is being discussed in the meeting at the same time? Probably not, and there is a good reason for that.

In the first case, we were focusing willingly and intentionally on the meeting and 'listened' to everything that was being discussed. That is an example of active listening; hearing with an intention to understand and comprehend. When we actively listen to our colleagues in the meeting, it is natural that any background noise automatically gets ignored. You may still 'hear' them but you will only be listening to your colleagues and matters pertaining to the meeting.

Similarly, in the second example, you are trying to pay attention to the discussion that has caught your fancy. The trouble is, it is taking place outside the room. While somewhat loud, you will still need to pay close attention and focus in order to fully understand what is being spoken or discussed. While you try and actively listen to that, you will certainly miss out on quite a bit that is being discussed at the table.

Becoming an active listener is certainly a major step, but where you place and use your active listening skills matters equally as well. In this chapter, we will be focusing on finding out how active listening can help us out in resolving conflicts. We will also be looking at some of the most helpful tips and some common mistakes to further improve our active listening and strengthen our take on conflicts.

Active Listening - More Than Just Hearing

In the examples above, we saw how two similar situations had two different outcomes. That was perhaps the easiest example I could come up with, and I believe every professional would be able to relate to these examples. The above examples were just to get you started in the right direction.

As a part of my training quite some time ago, I was taught how to master the art of active listening. At first, it made no sense to me as active listening and listening sounded like pretty much the same thing. It was only after I started to learn more that I realized there is a world of difference between what we call listening and what active listening is.

Listening, or hearing, is broadly similar. You hear something, comprehend some of the meaning and that's it. When it comes to active listening, not only are you listening with intent, you are also trying to identify the important areas as the person speaks. You will have different body language that highlights your interest. From positive eye contact to a gentle smile or a nod at times, followed by the usual "uh-huh," all of these contribute towards active listening.

Through active listening, we get to make the other person feel that we value their opinion or whatever it is that they have to say. Our body language, our concern for them and their problems, and our unbreaking attention towards them can allow them to open up further and hence provide you with important or crucial information at times as well. In cases of conflict between two friends, you may not be able to find out the root cause if you are not trying to make the other person feel as if you are truly concerned for them and are willing to hear them out.

It is only natural that we humans need someone to hear us out at times. Sometimes, sharing is indeed the best way to move forward and resolve issues. However, not everyone is willing to hear us out. It takes an active listener to play his/her role in order to make us feel like we are important and that our issues are worth their time. Trust me, it truly helps to hear someone out or be heard by someone when we run into issues.

It is through active listening that you gain some level of trust and a bit of understanding with conflicting parties. It is through active listening that these parties may actually turn to you and divulge information regarding their issues, interests, or needs. Through this transfer of information, you can quickly resolve conflict and perhaps even take away the tension within the air. With that said, it is quite tricky to master active listening, as we shall now see.

To begin with, there are far too many distractions which often, and very easily, derails us from the objective. Think about the last time your friend approached you regarding a problem. Your friend probably asked you to hear him/her out. While your friend started to share their issues and problems, I wish for you to try and recall which of the following situations you related to. It is vital that you remain honest with yourself to make the most of the test.

During the course of your friend's monologue, you:

- Eagerly waited for your friend to finish so that you can begin your story and explain how you have gone through the same thing.

- Related to some incident that is somewhat the same and then waited for your turn to speak.

- You paid attention to what your friend had to say and you already had a few good ideas ready despite the fact that your friend did not specifically ask for advice.

- You heard the entire version thoroughly without uttering a word to fully understand the issue and then spoke accordingly.

Let me rest you assured; there is no wrong answer here. All of these are natural responses that we can come up with. However, it is now a good time to understand that one of these is always going to be a bit more productive, especially when it comes to resolving conflict: the last scenario. That is a prime definition of active listening. It is a form of hearing where you understand someone else first before proceeding to have yourself understood.

For anyone who has ever worked in a customer service department, it is very easy to relate to what active listening is. Time and again, the customer service representatives are trained, taught and tasked to use their active listening skills to allow greater communication between the customer and the representative.

There are those who would question how active listening is any different than "listening closely," and they have every right to do so. To an untrained mind, listening and active listening would play the same role. For those within fields such as customer services, psychology, or any other walk of life where you get to deal with issues faced by people, it would be a completely different thing.

Imagine an irate customer, calling in for a complaint that he has already raised twice. So far, he has yet to see any progress and, naturally, he is not at all pleased. The minute someone picks up the call and greets him, the customer loses his calm and composed nature. The customer is not ready to listen to anything this representative has to say or offer, and wishes to speak to the supervisor.

Here are my points for you to consider:

- How does screaming/venting out at the representative help?

- Does the customer actually get anything productive done by asking for a supervisor?

- What should this representative do in such a situation?

Customer representatives get to face numerous calls where customers would call in to register their complaints, claims or feedback. Addressing these is no ordinary task as one needs to truly keep his/her ears wide open and portray a significant use of active listening.

It is through active listening that the representative will fully understand what the customer has to say. Tiny details can matter and all it takes is one simple distraction, and before you know it, the representative either records the information wrong or asks the customer once again. Either way, it is not going to sound professional nor comforting to the customer that they were not being paid the attention they deserve.

This would lead the customer to grow irate, a state where the customer would be irritated and may resort to unpleasant tones and anger. What may have started as a perfectly ordinary call ended up being an escalation. The entire scenario that could have been avoided is now one that requires a supervisor. Not only did you lose your trust and rapport that you may have made, but you also ended up taking a hit on your monthly performance report.

Throughout the issue, there are a few things to observe:

1. Let's say the customer was irate because he/she was not fully informed about the waiting period to receive a resolution. This information could only be acquired through active listening. In any other manner, it would have been impossible to find out the issue.

2. Listening actively to the customer's concerns and worries not only allows the representative to build trust and rapport, but also allows one to head towards a solution.

3. Active listening can resolve almost every situation, even if the customer and the representative are hundreds or thousands of miles away.

You can slice it in any manner, the fact remains the same: without active listening, the above example would have never been solved.

Active listening can greatly improve your chances of learning and identifying the root cause of the entire conflict. Whether the conflict involves loud arguments, silent disagreements, or even frowns, the longer we allow conflict to sustain, the bigger the problems get. Instead, stop for a second and think it through. Think if you need to remain quiet and allow someone else to speak first.

More than half of the issues between married couples are solved if one of the two remains silent and listens to the other party with an intent to understand the problem and resolve the same. Yes, it does take a bit of practice and it is not easy, especially if ego gets in the way. However, for the sake of the relationship, and to master the art of conflict resolution, we need to take the higher road and learn how to be selfless.

Just by lending an ear to your spouse, you are comforting your significant other as they are reassured of your presence and support. To make things even better for yourself and the other party, you will need to ensure the following:

- Remain neutral - There is no reason for you to pick a side, even if the conflicting parties involve you on one side. Learn how to remain neutral and weigh both sides on their merits.

- Remain non judgmental - It is very easy for us to jump to conclusions. Assumption can sometimes be misleading and can lead to grave consequences. Try to steer clear of your instincts and judgements, and allow yourself to fully hear the other person without judging them.

- Verbal/Non-verbal signs - Depending on the situation, use the appropriate verbal or physical gestures to indicate that you are listening to the speaker with attention. Maintaining consistent eye contact is one of the finest ways to let the other person know that they are being paid attention to. Use facial expressions to show sadness, sorrow, surprise or happiness.

- Ask questions - Ensure that you ask relevant questions, which are free from any criticism, sarcasm or judgements. These questions further strengthen the rapport and understanding between you and the speaker. Use both open-ended and closed-ended questions to filter out required information. The more you learn of the issue, the better you can resolve it.

- Asking for any kind of clarification - There is no harm is asking the speaker to clarify things. It is perfectly natural for us to misunderstand something or be unable to make any sense of something. Asking to clarify a statement or a word lets the other person know you are paying attention and trying to fully understand the situation.

These are definitive qualities of active listening and, when applied effectively, can greatly assist in diffusing the tension and moving productively towards a resolution.

Important Aspects to Remember

While there is no universal manner for every one of us to follow, there are a few things which are generally seen in practice throughout the world. Therefore, I will focus on those as I too practice the same when the time is right. These qualities and elements about active listening help me and almost every professional who gets to deal with clients, customers, and patients and tries to identify, understand, and resolve conflicts.

Just a few lines ago, we went through a few important aspects of active listening. Active listening, through applying the useful methods, allows us to steer clear of 'bad' listening habits. These are exactly the opposite of active listening habits and characteristics.

Here are some of the commonly identified bad listening habits:

- Lack of respect for the person/speaker - There are moments where we may be at the listening end of a monologue being delivered by someone we do not know or like. In such circumstances, we must learn to brush our personal feelings aside and pay attention to the speaker and respect their feelings and opinions.

- Interruptions - It is annoying and, at times, rude to interrupt the speaker. This can escalate the situation and add yet another reason to the conflict that is clearly brewing. Try to remain silent and be a good listener.

- Avoiding eye contact - Avoiding eye contact is usually perceived as a bad sign by anyone. Imagine trying to speak to a person who is looking everywhere else apart from you. Initially, this may not bother you, but it will eventually start feeling like the person is trying to avoid you.

- Rushing the speaker to hurry up - I admit that there are moments where you may feel bored, exhausted, tired, or even feel like you are losing your focus. This generally happens when the speaker is discussing matters which may not be related to you or may seem too general or repetitive in nature. Try not to rush the speaker in any manner as this may create a bad impression.

- Ignoring the bits you may not understand - It is natural for us to just try and skip the parts we did not understand. We always tend to find a way to connect the dots. Often, we end up getting it wrong, and that can lead to problems. Instead of ignoring such parts, ask!

Clearly, bad listening habits are the perfect mixture of components to cook a disastrous situation. What may start off as a simple conversation can very well end in a quarrel or fight.

We can safely draw a conclusion that active listening can indeed save us from unnecessary issues and actually lead towards a productive and effective way of solving matters. Taking the same conclusion further, we can apply active listening to quite a few areas of our lives to further amplify the benefits and keep most conflicts at bay, if not all.

1. Active listening in relationships - Listening to your significant other or partner allows you to further strengthen your relationship. By actively listening to the problems and opinions, free from prejudice, bias or judgments, you can understand the other person's point of view. This validates the speaker as well, hence making them speak in more detail. Through active listening, you always let your partner know that you recognize their importance and understand that the conversation is more about them than you. The fewer the conflicts, the happier the couple.

2. Active listening at work - Listening actively at work can help you save yourself from quite a few conflicts and problems. This is true especially if you are in a management role where you may have to deal with quite a few colleagues at work. Through active

listening, you will learn how to understand matters, resolve conflicts, and arrive at productive and effective resolutions easily.

3. Active listening when meeting new people - This should be self-explanatory. Whether you are interested in getting to know more about a person, or you are tasked with the duty to interview people for a job, you will need to rely on your active listening skills quite a lot.

There are countless situations and scenarios where active listening will come into play and help you avoid conflict. If you practice this unique skill properly, you may very well be referred to by many within your social circle as the person to approach when conflict arises.

Active listening is the most important addition to your toolkit. Through active listening, you can greatly reduce the stress, tension, and intensity of the moment. Resolving situations between two parties or resolving conflicts between you and someone else may require you to use different strategies. With that said, however, the first step in either case would be active listening. One of us will need to listen actively and draw out a conclusion to identify the problem. Only then can we proceed to find mutually benefiting ground.

Chapter 3:
Recognizing Different Perspectives (And Learning to Accept One's Mistakes)

The last chapter mostly focused on the all-important trait of active listening. We saw how essential active listening is, and to some of us, it may have been a bit of a surprise to know just how easily conflicts can be avoided just by listening to the other party with intent and purpose.

It is certainly hard to get into practice, but once you get the hang of things, active listening will become a routine habit. It is one powerful trait to begin with, but it's not the only one.

Coming up in this chapter, we will learn how to understand and recognize different perspectives. We will look at some examples to see how different perspectives, when realized and worked upon, can help change the scenario and the outcome. We will also take a tough step to admit and accept our mistakes, when and where found. Combine these two brilliant steps, and you are moments away from ending the chaotic conflict between friends, family members, and even colleagues and seniors at work.

The 'Why' and the 'How'

Here is one of the most quoted examples on earth:

"A person places an empty glass on the table and pours in water until it reaches the halfway mark. Is the glass half-empty or half-full?"

This example is used in many lectures and seminars as a prime example. It is easy to relate to and allows us to think it through. So how does this example work and why exactly are we looking at this example instead of discussing more ways to deal with conflict? Let us see just why this example is important.

There are only two answers to the question above:

- Half-Empty

- Half-Full

Surprisingly, both the answers are right. If both the answers are right, then why ask the question in the first place? That is to highlight one small yet significant detail: the difference of perspective.

To you, the glass may be half-empty, which is perfectly fine. To me, it is half-full, which is correct as well. However, our perspectives are different. We are looking at the same thing with two unique perspectives. What is even more surprising is the fact that our perspectives cannot change the scenario. The glass contains half-a-glass of water, and that is the middle point we both agree upon. The only issue is that one of us is more focused on the lack of water while the other is focused on lack of space.

If both of us were to change our perspectives, just a little, we both may realize that we are looking at the same thing. The content within the glass does not change with either perspective and hence, the needless conflict can easily end by changing our perspective and looking at the situation through someone else's view.

Conflict arises in any place, between any relationship, and at any given time when there is a difference of opinion. In most cases, contradicting or varying opinions are the products of different perspectives. To one person, buying a house may be a priority. To their spouse, maybe an apartment is a better way to go about things. Both are looking for the same ultimate goal; to have a roof of their own. Instead of spending numerous hours arguing with each other, a more logical way would be to settle down and discuss matters like adults and resolve the issues accordingly.

Of course, in most cases, we are quick to jump to conclusions. We assume that our point of view is correct while the other party is talking nonsense. Fair enough, but when was the last time we stopped for a brief moment and thought, "What if I am wrong? What if the other party is actually right?"

The day you stop and think that is the day you start moving into the right direction. The problem lies in the fact that none of us will be ready to accept that we are wrong. There are people who will consider this equal to losing or admitting defeat. That is absolutely absurd and unnecessary, as human beings can make mistakes. Mistakes are what make us humans as we make them and then learn from them.

Unfortunately, some members of the society make it a point of honor or take it a little too personal if they are asked to admit their mistakes. The only reason that happens is because they lack emotional intelligence and are otherwise beyond worry or care.

Emotional intelligence is defined as the ability of identifying one's own emotions and manage those as well as the emotions of others. It is the study that basically looks at what pushes an intelligent, well-educated person into making blunders as well as what drives a person with significantly lower education to make highly intelligent decisions.

This study erupted in the 1980s. This new field of studies led to the idea of Emotional Intelligence (EQ). Where the IQ measures a person's intelligence by observing the way he/she processes information to arrive to a decision, the EQ revolves more around the emotional front and how one would process emotions of one's own self and others around him/her.

There was a time when I used to think this study was just a waste of time, until I met some real-life examples and realized just how important the existence of IQ and EQ is. A person may have an incredibly high IQ number on the card. He may be able to solve extremely difficult calculations and problems in a matter of seconds. Surely, a foolish decision on his part would seem nothing more than bad luck or a rare probability.

Do not be too sure on that just yet. If the person possesses a low EQ, there is every chance that the person is unable to manage emotions and learn how to control them. Uncontrolled emotions can often lead to quite a few problems, many leading to conflicts.

A simple misunderstanding about conflict is that it takes at least two people to have a conflict. If you are someone who believes that, here's my question to you. Do you not find yourself within a conflict where you are questioning or doubting your own capability, judgment, and are questioning whether you should take a step or not?

It is only natural for us to be in conflict with our own ideas, steps and judgments. We often criticize ourselves when faced with consequences, with the infamous line, "I knew I shouldn't have done that!"

Most of these conflicts that we manage to drag ourselves into are caused by uncontrolled and unchecked emotions. If that seems to be the case, you may have low EQ, which is why it may be difficult for you to manage your emotions properly.

A low EQ can certainly cause quite a few problems, chief among which is the inability to admit one's own mistake. Owing to the little to no capability of managing emotions, you might end up taking steps like shutting yourself out, feeling yourself to be isolated or targeted by everyone, and no one likes that.

You may develop a false perception that the world is against you and that no one understands you. Rest assured that there is a good chance your close ones can see things better than you can. The only reason you haven't done the same is because of your inability to manage your emotions.

Instead of taking things personally and being offended right away, try and remain calm. Pay attention to what exactly is bothering your beloved members of the family or friends. Try and view things from their perspective for a change. You might be in for a surprise to find out just how wrong you were looking at things.

A good judge is one that takes both sides into account, measures them on merit and arrives at a verdict accordingly. Only then can a verdict be declared as just. By only looking at things one way or favoring the side one is a little inclined too, it would be a biased judgement and may end up doing more harm than good.

View all the angles carefully and see how your words or actions affect those around you. See if you truly gain something from what you are doing or if you are losing more than you can manage to lose. Oh, and the low EQ? You can increase that at the same time as well. This then takes away the "I can't help it! I have a low EQ!" excuse which I know quite a few people end up with.

To get started on the right track, here are some great tips to increase your EQ levels.

1- Practicing the Art of Self-Awareness

The point is simple; you cannot expect to get better at things without knowing what they are all about. Throughout our lives, no one told us how important self-awareness really is. Without it, we are like a boat at the mercy of the sea. The boat has no sail so it is pretty much riding the waves. You cannot control the direction nor the intensity.

Self-awareness is what allows you to understand yourself and your own behavior. With self-awareness, you get to know yourself on three levels:

1. Knowing about what you are doing

2. Knowing how you feel about something

3. Things you did not or may not have known about yourself (the hardest part to conquer)

These may seem easy, right? You might be thinking how on earth you wouldn't know what or who you are doing. The fact of the matter is that we live in times where we do not have any idea of what we are doing almost half the time. We are far too caught up in our world and we fail to notice how our mind needs a bit of a time out.

One of the leading causes of conflicts and a major contributor to our lack of conflict resolving abilities is the fact that we are indulged 24/7 in our cell phones, emails, social profiles, etc. We rarely take time out for ourselves, thus affecting our mind and its cognitive power. A stressed mind, or one that is starving for a break, will perform poorly in conflicts.

First step, take some time off from cell phones, computers, and laptops. Remove the unnecessary distractions from your life. Find time to engage in healthy social activities like meeting friends instead of texting them.

You may be surprised to know this, but our mind needs a bit of solitude as well. Where possible, use a bit of meditation to allow your mind to re-center your focus and gain back the lost edge. You will need all of that in order to be a good listener and be better at resolving conflict.

A distracted mind can never prove to be efficient or effective when it comes to performing a task, even if it is a conflict of the smallest magnitude. While meditation helps, it is also beneficial to practice a few stress relieving exercises, such as breathing techniques. These can ensure you do not take actions resulting from stress, as these can certainly strain matters further. A quick breathing exercise can also ensure your blood pressure levels remain calm and you remain composed and focused.

Next, we have to come to terms with how we feel. It is a vital step to move forward and increase our self-awareness. Quite a few of us either remain ignorant to what we feel or we simply do not accept our feelings for what they are. Accepting your emotions allows you to pursue a more constructive path towards dealing with matters accordingly. Rejecting our feelings or not being aware of them may end in us taking steps which may lead us back where we started from.

This will also lead you to start noticing things you may have not noticed or taken into account otherwise. You may discover things such as triggering points, irrational hatred, or aspects which make you agitated. The more you know about them, the better you can plan ahead and manage them accordingly.

All of these contribute significantly towards your self-awareness, which is an integral part of better emotional intelligence. That being said, it is certainly not the only aspect we need to take into account. There are other aspects out there which we need to look into to further understand and improve emotional intelligence.

2- *Knowing how to channel your emotions*

We live in this bubble of misconception that we can control our emotions. I hate to burst that bubble, but the fact of the matter is this: emotions are natural, and we can only control how we react to these.

All the emotions we feel and experience only trigger a response, which forces us to pay attention to something that is seemingly important right then and there. This is exactly why anger is a destructive emotion, as most of us may fail to direct it and respond to it appropriately. A simple change of perspective can shift that anger and allow us to use it to correct the mistake and improve upon the general situation.

3- *Knowing and learning how to motivate one's own self*

There are times where we feel absolutely lost. We rarely keep track of time and are otherwise engaged and immersed in activities which we either like or find favorable. Notice that when doing something we like or prefer, we often feel motivated by the excitement or joy of it.

Motivating our own self is quite important. Every now and then, we need a reminder that we, as individuals, trust our own capabilities and trust our instincts. Motivate yourself as often as you can. You need all that positive energy in order to lead a better lifestyle.

The more motivated you feel, the better you can manage your emotions and improve your overall emotional intelligence.

4- Identifying emotions found in others

So far, we have been rather focused on what goes on within our mind. To further help yourself and increase your emotional intelligence, it is also wise to start noticing how others feel around you.

Learn how each action from you affects them. There may be moments where the other person feels chuffed about something you did, which is good. On the other hand, there may be moments where something you did brought quite a bit of disturbance within the air and the tensions and emotions run high. Instead of avoiding that, learn how to identify these. See how the other person reacts to it.

A sign of a healthy relationship is that you will be able to quickly identify what your partner feels at any given moment. Learn how to recognize and respect the emotions of one another. Use empathy as your main trait to further ease the situation.

Sharing your thoughts with others and listening to what they have to say can greatly diffuse tensions, remove conflicts and allow for better emotional intelligence to make its way through the scenario.

Here's a simple example. Instead of finding faults in others, stop and think if you are truly without flaws. It is very much possible that your partner has already accepted you for who you are and as you are. If that is the case, it is only fair enough that you reciprocate the affection by accepting them the way they are. And the best way to do that is by using empathy; a trait known to many but mastered by few.

5 - Add values to your emotions

This tip is slightly different from the rest, but it is quite effective. We all know our emotions to a certain extent. Let us assume that we have learned how to gain the finest emotional intelligence and we are feeling all set to lead our team to newer heights by teaching them how to be more motivated towards work, better at conflict resolution, and generate quite a lot of sales.

Everything seems fine, except for the fact that most of our product is being manufactured by a group of under-privileged workers, working on extremely low wages, somewhere far off. All that emotional intelligence, then, stands null and void.

Infuse values by first knowing what you truly value and what is valued by others. Ensure you add along with your emotions honesty, transparency, integrity, loyalty, and any other qualities that you think are important. If you are motivating someone, be sure to promote these qualities with them as well. There is no point in motivating someone to achieve a desired result if it means breaking the law or blurring the lines a bit.

How Does EQ Help, Then?

Emotional intelligence is underrated, misunderstood, and frankly an overlooked skill. While one may have an IQ level north of 130, which is considered as superior, they may still end up making some of the weirdest decisions on earth. We learned previously that EQ is our ability to handle emotions as they come.

Imagine that due to low sales, or some technical fault, the CEO of Apple decides to call it a day and throw in the towel. Surely, the news of Apple shutting down would rattle the world, but would that be a justified decision? Certainly not. That would only show how bad of an EQ the person had which led him to make such a rash decision.

Through the five methods mentioned above, you will be better at making decisions and resolving conflicts. How? Let's take a look at this example.

Example 1:

A person working within a customer service department of a large corporate organization is earning a good salary. The guy is working hard and is married happily as well. However, this person is not exactly seeing eye-to-eye with his immediate boss.

Every now and then, both men are seen arguing over whose fault the last issue was and how it could have been handled, and as usual, both end the argument abruptly by walking away from the floor.

This is growing into a bit of an issue. The senior manager decides to set the differences aside and get to the bottom of the situation once and for all.

Using active listening, empathy, a focused mind and a will to resolve matters, the senior manager hears each one of them individually. It does not take long for him to figure out that both are right in their own perspective but one has a better solution for the other.

Once the tempers have settled, the manager calls both of them inside his office and allows them to listen to what each had to say. Normally, this conversation would have been going on for quite some time, but this time around, with the absence of temper, both the parties finally heard each other out and now understood each other better.

The employee admitted the mistake and appreciated that the senior manager acknowledged his stance as well. This served as motivation that his efforts were being noticed. At the same time, the immediate boss also appreciated that his suggestions were eventually declared as the better path and that the employee under him happily agreed to follow the same.

What started out as a conflict ended rather easily with just a light discussion and everyone walked away from the issue with a smile.

Moral: Either involve someone who knows both sides and can remain neutral or learn how to handle emotions better by acknowledging the other perspective.

The boss was right, in the end, but the unfriendly tone he used in previous conflicts did not help. The employee was a hard-working employee but the retaliatory temper stood in the way of progress. Once both the parties were able to look past the differences and manage their emotions more productively, a conclusive result was reached.

Perspectives certainly change and it is very easy for us to find ourselves at the receiving end. Instead of retaliating, let the other person speak completely. It is very possible that the other party might be right or may even have a better approach to a problem.

Perspectives can honestly cause quite a lot of issues, especially if you are working with a number of people. Being a member of a team or leading one equally require you to remain neutral and have a grip on your emotions. Do not let your emotions make decisions for you which you may later on regret, nor allow your ego to get in the way.

Relations at home, work, and within communities can easily be created, strengthened or destroyed, all depending on how well you handle your emotions and allow others to share their perspectives. Being there for them does not only mean that you are physically there, but it also means that you are ready to hear their version of the story and accept mistakes of your own, if and when found.

Resolving conflicts is never easy as it does take quite a bit of your ability to set your ego, status, knowledge, and understanding aside to make room for someone else's perspective. Just accepting one's own mistake can at times eliminate most of the issues right away. The rest may just be a bit of, "I do apologize for the inconvenience and hopefully you will not see that happen ever again," and it should do the magic for you.

Tip: If you use the above sentence, be sure to mean it. Trust me, it helps if you do!

Chapter 4:
Communication Skills You Need to Have In Your Toolbox

So far, we have seen what conflict is and how easily it can be triggered. We have gone through some chapters about being an active listener and being open to other perspectives, learning about emotional handling capabilities and a little more. To be honest, that is just scratching the surface. The actual meat of conflict resolution starts now.

Through the last two chapters, I have mentioned ways to be on the receiving end and exercise tolerance and acceptance. Now, it is time for us to look into matters which may take place while hearing the other party or after you have the chance to respond to the situation.

Remember how emotions are just emotions and what matters is how we respond to them? Keep that in mind, as most conflict resolution revolves around that idea. It is this simple line that will make more sense as we progress further.

I may not be wrong to mention that conflicts are generally created due to miscommunication. It is normally a word, a sentence, an opinion or a gesture that is either misunderstood or deliberate in nature that provokes the other party to retaliate and take action which they see fit. I have been in quite a few situations where it was just a simple misunderstanding, or a lack of awareness on my end, and things quickly could have gone bad. All it took was for me to immediately realize my mistake and show body language that expressed my regret and use words which were appropriate for the occasion. What I did was effective communication; any other kind and I would have ended up with a black eye and a bit of a tough time explaining to my spouse what had happened.

All of us are natural communicators. The most effective communicators, to everyone's surprise, are babies. Why? It is sheerly because they know nothing more than crying to express they want something. Immediately, we quit everything and start attending to the needs of the child. Crying is the only way babies can communicate until they reach a certain age and start mimicking words that they often hear. This is the best and perhaps the purest form of communication because:

- It is down-right honest

- It is free of any bias

- It is conveyed without hindrance

- It holds no hidden agendas

It is only when we start growing that we lose the effectiveness and focus on ways to demand something without actually asking for it. Not long after, we learn how to get things we want, even if we have to lie for them or make up stories. The vicious cycle then starts and never ends. Lying, deceiving, hiding our feelings, or even refusing to acknowledge feelings leads us to lose our effectiveness from communication.

Now, as adults, we realize that we have not been an effective communicator for quite some time. Learning all that now may be harder than it sounds. Not only do you have to learn how to be frank, straight-forward and honest, but you also need to learn how to tolerate the response you may get for telling someone they are not working properly, or that a dress your spouse bought you is not what you expected. That is quite a monumental task.

Fortunately, there are ways we can learn how to do all that and do it in a way that does not harm anyone's feelings. Of course, we do not wish to be caught in a situation where we are trying to resolve a conflict and end up being a contributor instead. This chapter will focus solely on what exactly effective communication is and why is it important for everyone to master. We will find out just what it takes to become an effective communicator and also learn how this quality can help us resolve conflicts that may have already arisen.

Effective Communication 101

Communication - defined as a simple flow of information from person A to person B, from one party to another and so on, and so forth. It is both verbal and non-verbal in form and exists as a vital part of our lives.

It is absolutely wrong, and somewhat naive, to say that communication is based on words alone. If that were the case, sign-language would have never been a mode of communication. Communication goes far beyond the scope of words or how they are used. Communication involves your body gestures, your facial expressions, your mental and physical response to situations. The list can go on and on.

With that said, there is a massive difference between communication and effective communication. It is often the lack of the latter which leads people and parties into conflicts. Owing to the lack of skills on one side, a conflict quickly stirs up and leads to harsher outcomes. These conflicts are mostly unintentional, but there are occasions where these are intentional and deliberate.

We will not be looking into the deliberate issues, but we will certainly look into the defining characteristics of an effective communicator. After all, our objective now is to move ahead and resolve conflicts.

There are quite a few components which one needs to learn and exercise in order to become an effective communicator. The benefits of effective communication are easy to spot and feel, and this trait can certainly help you in many areas of life.

Example 2

For this example, we will be looking at a typical error in communication and how that can lead to a conflict. This example is to show just how crucial and beneficial effective communication can be.

Scenario 1:

Mr. May called his employee and asked him to fetch the file he was assigned yesterday. Moments later, when the employee arrived with a bunch of files, all hell broke loose.

Mr. May, as a boss, was already under quite a bit of pressure and was handling a lot of important matters. Time is a luxury that he always could not afford to lose. Now, being presented with more than a few files, he lost his temper and yelled at the employee.

The employee tried to interrupt and explain why he did what he did but Mr. May was past the point of allowing anyone else to speak. The conflict that could have been avoided now caused panic and a chaotic scene, all because of a miscommunication.

If you are trying to locate what exactly was miscommunicated here, you may wish to read the next scenario first!

Scenario 2:

Mr. May called his employee and asked him to fetch **the red file containing important financial data of the firm** which was assigned to him yesterday. The employee swiftly glanced through the number of files which came in yesterday and picked out the red one with the correct label on it.

Moments later, Mr. May had the file at his desk, and appreciated the swiftness shown by the employee. The employee left with a smile and Mr. May carried on working.

The Big Takeaway: Clear and effective communication saved both members of the office from an unnecessary conflict. In the earlier scenario, the boss failed to think through and gave a general directive. He failed to provide specifics and hence the employee was left in a bit of a puzzled state. To ensure his boss got what he wanted, he took all the files he received a day earlier to eliminate the awkward chance of presenting the wrong file before the boss. Sure enough, this backfired drastically and led to flaring tempers and unnecessary conflict.

This example is quite a common sight. Anyone can easily relate to such instances in life where we may have heard something and instead of clarifying, we followed the directives that led to a conflict. However, the above example only shows **how a conflict could have been avoided**, but what if you are already in the middle of a conflict and need to resolve that instead? Equip yourself with a notebook and a pen, and take notes as this will include quite a few things for you to understand and practice.

Honesty

I would love to meet the person who coined the phrase "Honesty is the best policy," because it is indeed the finest quality to have these days.

Whenever someone mentions honesty, I honestly recall a line I picked up from a movie. It may seem like dialogue that was initially intended to be humorous, but it certainly got me thinking a little deeper.

"Me? I'm dishonest, and a dishonest man you can always trust to be dishonest. Honestly. It's the honest ones you want to watch out for, because you can never predict when they're going to do something incredibly... stupid." - Captain Jack Sparrow/ Pirates Of The Caribbean: Curse of the Black Pearl

That is true. Being honest is not easy to begin with, and if by some magic you have learned how to be 100% honest, you may end up doing things which were either uncalled for or absolutely rude.

Practicing honesty and being honest comes with quite a challenge. Not only do you need to learn how to be honest, but you will also need to find out ways to fashion your statements in a manner that does not offend anyone and yet conveys the message clearly and effectively.

Imagine a wife telling her husband that he is not working hard to make a suitable living. The wife is being honest, but the way she chose to be honest could have been slightly different. This way, it is blunt, rude and could easily start an argument.

Instead, pause for a second and think things through. The spouse has had a long day at work. You probably have no idea of the things he/she may have had to put up with, just to make ends meet. Be an effective communicator and start by being honest about how his/her input greatly helps. Then, put in a bit of a concern that all of you can surely search for better alternatives which pay better with the amount of work the spouse currently puts in.

If you appreciate the effort and remain honest, there is virtually no reason for anyone to debate, argue, or fight. Your message is conveyed loud and clear that you care for your spouse and consider that he/she can earn more elsewhere for exactly the same effort. You can then observe the reaction and share how you wish to make things better by chipping in somehow. Perhaps, things may actually work for the best, but it is a subtle way to convey a message effectively without raising any alarms.

Emotional awareness

Much like the emotional intelligence, which we discussed above, it is vital to have emotional awareness as it greatly allows you to be a better, more effective communicator. It is almost the same as emotional intelligence, with only a slight difference. Here, we are focusing more on the general awareness about emotions and feelings of everyone instead of our own.

Understanding emotions is not exactly an art. It is a skill that can easily be mastered by all. Then, the excuse of, "How was I supposed to know?" does stand redundant. If you do not believe me, visit your favorite bar the next time you can and try to observe people within the bar.

You will easily be able to read most of the faces and find out what they may be feeling. You may not hit the bullseye every time, but there is a good chance you will get the general picture of how a person may be feeling. That is because all of us are built with the ability to tell what another person is feeling.

Use this ability when communicating. This is vital to ensure that you do not end up passing comments, opinions, or ideas that may otherwise offend the other person or are absolutely inappropriate for the occasion.

If someone has suffered an accident, it is understood that one would show up with flowers and get well soon cards to wish the injured a speedy recovery. Imagine the horror if someone comes up and decides to talk about how accidents kill and how thousands die every now and then. Not only are you creating a sense of discomfort, but you are also making yourself look ridiculous for being insensitive.

Pay attention to what the other party is feeling and use your communication skills accordingly. Use a comforting tone to let the other person know you care. While I truly believe there is no such thing as a wrong question, I do understand that every question has a place and a time. A misplaced or mistimed question may not be appropriate to ask then and there. You can certainly ask once the situation has changed.

Emotional awareness is a huge game changer for conflict resolutions as well. By carefully observing emotions in general, you can take a more pragmatic approach to resolve the issue in a tone that suits the occasion and words that communicate the solutions or concerns accordingly.

Bonus: With practice, emotional awareness can certainly help strengthen your relationships as well. It worked like a charm for quite a few of my close friends and the difference is phenomenal.

Problem Solving Skills

Okay, this one is not exactly a piece of cake or a walk in the park. You genuinely need to work on your problem solving skills, but the good news is that there are tons of methods you can use to improve.

Problem solving skills are some of the most common yet most difficult to acquire skills in existence. Where most of us feel like we can solve any problem, we often find ourselves running away from issues owing to our fears. Those fears draw their roots from our problem solving abilities, or lack thereof.

You are often faced with situations where conflicts are seemingly everywhere, but all it takes is one problem solver to resolve matters and arrive at a solution that conflicting parties might actually accept and compromise upon.

Learning and sharpening your problem solving skills can be arduous at first, but once you get the hang of things, you will soon feel the difference. Now, you would be more capable of solving complex problems within shorter spans of time. People will start looking up to you as their "go-to" person to seek advice on problems.

"So how exactly do I learn or practice problem solving skills?"

Well, that is fortunately the easier bit. Since we are concerned about effective communication, you can do some of these to help you solve problems more efficiently, without risking any damage or harm to you or to anyone else.

- Try and state your problems while acknowledging problems faced by others at the same time. If you are being bombarded with complaints, do not retaliate with complaints as well.

- Use silence when and where possible. It is your greatest strength and a solid indicator that you are willing to hear what the other party has to offer.

- Use an apologetic tone, or better yet apologize when possible.

- Do not dwell on the past - it is done and dusted. Focus on 'now' and the future.

- Try not to deviate from the topic.

- Find grounds of agreement - they are always there.

- Postpone the discussion to another session if things are clearly going the opposite way.

- Use positive verbal and body language. For any negative expressions or feelings, ensure to only use words.

Practicing these may take time and you might actually forget all of these when faced with a real-life conflict. It takes practice and quite a lot of it as well. Try to write these down, or try to memorize at least three of these to get started.

Stress Management

This is arguably the biggest hurdle in the way of progress. If there was ever a universal issue that I would personally like to eradicate, it would be stress. Stress is our body's response to a given situation. Managing stress is extremely vital for a healthy life, relationships, and overall well-being of a person.

Almost every conflict that arises brings forth a profound level of stress. Stress can then block your ability to think straight. If you are not thinking straight, you cannot be an effective communicator. Therefore, it is vital for everyone to be in their best state of mind, and the only way you can do that is to learn how to manage stress to a bare minimum.

Learning how to manage your stress can greatly allow you to remain active and be able to resolve most conflicts with finesse. I have written a separate book on stress management alone, which goes to show just how challenging this can be. However, as a good starting point, pick up a few quick breathing exercises. Alternatively, you can opt for stress toys such as the squishy ball, as these are mighty effective and can help in reducing spikes of stress that you may encounter.

Remember, the quicker you manage stress, the better you can solve issues for yourself and for those around you. With a stressed mind, you may never be able to fully utilize the skills and knowledge you possess effectively.

Collaboration and Negotiation Skills

Whether you are a law enforcer trying to diffuse a conflicting situation that can go bad at any given moment, or a member of a team that is at the edge of sanity over a matter of choices, you need some skills to avoid the bad.

Collaborating with others over professional or personal matters can be challenging, to say the least. With various opinions and perceptions, it does get difficult to be able to find a mutually benefitting ground when both you and the other members are trying to reign supreme or play the role of authority.

Collaboration is virtually impossible without negotiation. You need to know how you will negotiate with the other party and arrive at an agreement that is beneficial to both sides.

A simple example would see a person trying to buy a car from a private seller. The seller of the car is trying to sell the car off and add in a little extra to buy a new one. The buyer is looking to buy a car for a good price and hopefully save some money for any repairs that may be needed. Both parties have their aims and both will try their best to strike a deal. It is a conflict that takes place almost every single day.

If you have poor negotiation skills, you will either offer to buy the car for a ridiculously low price or you would simply not bother at all. In either case, you will most likely end up losing the money or the car itself, the choice is yours. If you are good at a bit of bargaining, you may offer a sum that is reasonable, followed with logical reasons to support the bid. The more sensible your reasons, the better the chance of being successful.

Similarly, when the law enforcing agencies are tasked with defusing a situation, they usually collaborate with other members of the team. Their precision and focus is unwavering, as all of them accept and acknowledge the objective as the only priority of the hour. All of them move swiftly and carefully to navigate through any hurdles. They are always equipped with the skills to negotiate a surrender. Trust me, it is far easier said than done.

Things can get out of hand quickly, but their sublime skills ensure that culprits voluntarily surrender and avoid creating a mess. That is sheerly down to the fact that their collaboration allowed them to work together as a team and with the subject of interest into a safer outcome while their negotiation skills ensured both the parties arrived at a logical conclusion.

There are times you may have to work with people you don't really like or prefer not to be around. In such cases, these skills can certainly help you resolve conflicts and manage the situation more productively. As a former student, I too had to work with many students whom I initially did not like, but it was later that I discovered that collaborating with them brought results I could have never hoped to achieve on my own.

Collaborating with others can deliver great results and allow you, or the team, to complete tasks far more effectively and efficiently. There is a reason why construction engineers work in perfect synch with architectural engineers, designers, and contractors to build a building from the ground up. Without their seamless collaboration, things would be all over the place. Someone may have already started working on the third floor while you are out there trying to lay the ground for the basement. It is all going to lead into a big messy situation and result into losses you cannot fathom.

Patience

Ah! Patience. Take a deep breath, relax and wait.

Patience is indeed a virtue. Those who exercise patience in times of distress certainly come out the other end as better people. Patience is what wears thin quickly in most of us. Incredibly, some have developed patience to a new height where it stands like an impenetrable fortress.

Patience can get you out of numerous situations of conflict. When someone may be busy yelling and screaming at the top of their lungs, your patience would allow you to overlook that and remain calm. Eventually, this person would start feeling guilty for being so rude and cave in. That is where you can easily explain your end of the story and clarify any issues right there and then.

Patience is a skill that I have valued the most. There are times when we feel like we are living in the worst situation possible. We feel insignificant and that all our efforts go in vain. To go through these difficult times, we need patience. The problem is that we cannot find patience within ourselves at times.

To build up on patience, try maintaining a diary. It certainly helps me to vent out all that I feel and allows me to remain calm and composed when things seem to get really hard. If you are someone who prefers to talk to friends, by all means do so. But, the ultimate objective is to increase our patience, and there is nothing that beats a good meditation session.

Meditate regularly and soon you will find your stress levels depleting and patience levels of unimaginable magnitude rising. It will take a bit of time, but once you start developing your patience, you can face any conflict without ever worrying about losing your temper.

Empathy

Yes, we have come across this term a few times now. Empathy, believe it or not, can work like a charm in any given situation. It is something that can help you out of a sticky situation and allow you to resolve conflicts more effectively. How?

To begin with, empathy is one great way to cut the tension in the air. With a friendly tone, a caring voice and a genuine sense of concern and care towards the other, the other party will most likely break down and vent their frustrations out. Psychologists use empathy every single day with various patients to get to the root of the problem.

Through empathy, people understand your intent and care, and hence start trusting you. When someone trusts you, they will surely pay attention to what you have to say. When conflicts emerge, you can provide valuable input and defuse the situation using empathy.

Empathy can work in relationships, with friends, with colleagues and almost anywhere that you can think of. Empathy is considered to be an important part of your conflict resolution toolbox as it greatly increases the chance of making a significant breakthrough and moving towards a resolution.

To get you started, start using words which show care and respect towards other fellow members. Phrases like "I understand" can cause a soothing effect on the other person, and that can greatly calm their nerves down. Everyone could use a bit of care every now and then, so why not be the one to provide them with that?

Positivity

Remaining positive in the middle of a conflict? I know this sounds incredibly tough. Take it from a person who does this for a living, and still finds it hard at times to cope with the issue at hand.

Positivity can certainly create an immediate sense of relief for quite a few, and it can equally bother others as well. While some may appreciate your positivity, others may question it.

When being positive about something, you must continue to remain friendly and hopeful about things which may seem impossible. Your positivity is contagious, and it can certainly have an effect on the other party. Pretty soon, the other person might start seeing things on the brighter side as well.

When listening to others ranting on about how their colleagues thought they were wrong, and how the boss was losing his temper for no reason, remain calm and positive. Use appropriate language and show them the brighter side of things.

An accident happened at work? "Well, look on the brighter side; it could have been worse."

Impartiality

As a team member, or a leader, you are often faced with issues at work where you will need to either take sides or resolve a situation by declaring one wrong and the other right. This exercise is a little tricky, but it gets a lot trickier if one side is comprised of a person or a group of people you like or know on a personal level. Choosing between two sides then is far too difficult.

The best way to move in such circumstances is to ensure that you remain impartial. Let both parties provide you with their arguments. Once you have heard both sides, arrive at a logical conclusion, purely based on merits, and let everyone know that you prefer to just stay neutral. This may be hard at first, but soon, people will place their trust in you to resolve conflicts should they ever arise again.

"What if I am a party in the conflict? How do I exercise impartiality then?"

First things first, make up your mind that you will resolve the issue and are willing to accept criticism, as long as it is justifiable and on merit. Keep your mind open towards the possibility that you may even be completely wrong, in which case you must be willing to make amends.

With such a mindset, share your opinions and thoughts in a mature manner and hear the other side out. If things are too complicated, involve someone else who can remain neutral. In either case, when you hear the other party and share your own issues, you can then draw a logical conclusion and hopefully arrive at a mutually agreeable ground to settle the conflict.

Apologize for your mistakes, if found wrong. Be willing to take responsibility for your actions and try not to go into the blame game. If you do so, it will be a never-ending vicious cycle where you will continue to take responsibility and throw the blame across the table, and the other side will do exactly the same as well.

Eloquence

It is nothing more than having a graceful way with words. It is what gives you that persona that everyone loves. It is the way you use words to instill a sense of authority and persuade almost anyone easily.

Using eloquence requires almost all of the above, combined! Yes, that is quite a tall order, but once you start to work on your speaking skills, you will soon be in a commanding position. You will be speaking and people will be listening with pure interest.

By using eloquent words and maintaining a graceful personality, there is no possible reason for any conflict to remain strong. Pretty soon, one of the parties will allow you to step in and resolve the issue.

Similarly, if you are caught within a conflict with your spouse, friend or colleague, exercise eloquence. Remain graceful and people will automatically feel uncomfortable using harsh tones or language. With these two elements out, resolving the remainder of the conflict is just one "Oh, I see" and "I am sorry about that!" away.

All of these 10 attributes and traits provide quite a bit of an 'oomph' when it comes to resolving conflicts. It is best that you exercise each of these individually as each may pose some challenges at times. You can use these to resolve almost every type of conflict, whether personal or professional.

Chapter 5:
Resolving Conflicts Like a Boss

Okay, maybe your first reaction was "Oh yes!" or "Finally!" but that may be wrong. Conflicts can never be resolved by being bossy. If anything, you only add fuel to the flame by being a stubborn boss, directing and dictating your terms and wishes, and then expecting everyone to follow. Naturally, there will be revolt and mutiny.

When I refer to the phrase "like a boss," what I really mean is to resolve conflicts like a professional: with authority. It is like throwing a perfect pitch, or parking the car to perfection; you were always good at it and therefore do this far too easily.

Similarly, if you can resolve a few conflicts, you will gain invaluable experience which you can then use to resolve even more conflicts. Soon afterwards, people will be looking up to you to resolve conflicts and get things sorted out between parties.

This chapter, for once, deals with you being the expert and being the mediator between two or more parties, bound to prove each other wrong.

How we will do so will require patience, practice, and a bit of in-depth knowledge about a few aspects. Let us not waste any time and get straight to business.

Resolving Matters Like a Pro!

I will break this into sections. There is no rule to state that you should follow these steps in chronological order. You can use them in any way you please or see fit. Obviously, every situation that arrives before you will be unique. There are moments where you may be involved right from the start. Then, there can be moments where you are asked to jump into the middle of an ongoing conflict. And finally, there will be times where your input will quite literally be nonexistent. These are usually when you are asked to step in right at the end of a conflict, and before you even get a chance to say something, the entire conflict is resolved.

See which ones apply to you best and work accordingly, as each one of these will help you resolve matters personally and professionally.

The "AAA"

I call this the triple 'A' approach. There is no rocket science involved here, as you shall now see what each of these represent:

- Ask

- Accept/Acknowledge

- Analyze

You do not necessarily need to do these in this specific order. It is possible that you may have already accepted the situation for what it is and are now trying to analyze the situation as a neutral member of the conflict.

In either case, using these three attributes can greatly help you in creating sense out of a conflict. It can help you to remain neutral and take necessary steps to resolve the issue.

To maintain your authority, ensure to use assertiveness. Keep in mind that there is a fine line between being assertive and being bossy. Try not to mix these two up as each will fetch separate results; we are more interested in the former.

Analyze the situation from both views. Try to find which of the two side holds a more valid argument. If it helps, try to write the points down. Once you have sorted this, be sure to ask the right questions to further clarify any doubts.

Asking questions should not be hard nor embarrassing. If anything, asking questions about something further allows the parties to realize that you are paying attention to them and that you care enough to ask them a question to clarify the issue.

Lastly, where needed, acknowledge the good work and accept the fact that there have been some errors and that you are happy to help everyone. It really provides a sense of relief to members of the party to know that someone is trying to work together to solve issues.

Once all is done, identify the issues over which the parties are in disagreement. Write those down separately and then work out a way to bring both parties to a mutually agreeable ground.

This works in quite a few cases, but not always. In such cases, you may need to add in a little more than just the three A's.

Share Your Feelings

There are perhaps a million ways we can express what we feel to someone we know, care about, and love. However, as of late, I have observed that this natural ability of expressing love, affection, and sentiments is deteriorating. Slice it any way you prefer, but that is an alarming thought on its own.

We get to see examples of such occasions every now and then. You may come across people who yell over a simple disagreement. You may read about people who were calm and laughing minutes ago and the next thing you know, they ended up beating someone to a pulp. Why do you think this happens?

There are multiple reasons for this, and one of them is the lack of ability to express feelings properly. Whether it is love or hatred, approval or rejection, we are facing a hard time conveying this across the table.

I used to hide my feelings from a lot of people. I always thought that my opinions might end up being the exact opposite of the other person, and that it might upset them. The best course then was to stay quiet and go with the flow. I was so wrong!

Let me put it this way: the more you set aside your feelings, the more you burden your mind. One fine day, when you least expect it, you will lose your temper almost immediately and later on regret the entire fiasco.

Here's a more practical approach; share! Be honest to yourself and to the other person and start sharing what you truly feel. It is also a great way to manage stress. Share what you truly feel and respect what the other member may feel at the same time.

Conflicts are usually a result of a miscommunication. By taking the 'mis' away from communication, you are ideally left with clear ways to convey messages, information, and share feelings accordingly. Now, there is no reason in existence which may pave the way for conflict.

Whether trying to resolve personal, individual matters or trying to resolve a conflict at work, learn how to share your feelings honestly and encourage others to do the same. As long as everyone maintains composure and shares in a manner that is neither combative nor offensive, it should be fine.

Share Your Plan

You have given something a lot of thought and have come up with a plan. You have everything laid out before you and you are all set to execute the plan accordingly. However, at the last minute, someone you hold dear decides to show their reservations or objections to your plan. This certainly puts you in a bit of a tough spot.

While you always have the option of ignoring this person and continuing with your plan, it will only cause more problems in the future. Instead, try to share your plan with the other person. Let them know what you have decided to do and how it will benefit you and others around you.

I do not expect myself to be 100% correct every single time, which is why I prefer sharing my ideas with my spouse. I am always open to suggestions as I truly believe a fresh mind and a new perspective might actually allow me to revisit some ideas and make them even better.

Similarly, if you share your ideas and plan of action, you may acquire some ideas and gain some valuable feedback as well. If needed, you can easily modify the plan to make it better for everyone.

With that said, there are some points where this is just not an option. These are points that you are not at all ready to take any advice or suggestion for. In such cases, it is best to highlight these straight away in a professional and graceful manner. There is no reason to act like a boss and demand such pointers to be carried out at all costs.

If you are hoping to have some part of the plan carried out exactly the way you like, expect some demands from the opposite members of the party as well. With just a little compromise at both ends, you can eventually arrive at a solid agreement.

Always show signs or use words to encourage others to participate and share their demands or wishes as well. By allowing them to take part in the activity or the resolution, you are certain to arrive at a fair conclusion rather quickly.

The Alternatives

Mr. 'A' has come up with a good idea. It shows promising preliminary results. Some of the ideas provided, however, do seem a little vague.

At the same time, Mr. 'B' has come up with a plan that seems more promising, but the idea isn't exactly as bright as it may sound on the surface.

Where do you think you would go? Would you go on to support Mr. 'A' or would you prefer the approach by Mr. 'B'? What if you wanted a bit of this and a bit of that to create a third option where both the parties seemingly get what they want and everybody leaves happy? Obviously, the last one sounds like a more viable solution.

Every situation, regardless of how tough it may be, can have one alternative, if not more. Whether you are dealing with a conflict at home or at work, there is always a better alternative resolution out there that is waiting to be discovered. All you need is a mind that is willing to move past the arguments and the hassle and look for a solution.

Alternate solutions can often save you heaps of money, especially in commercial situations. As a firm, you may be tempted to follow the trend and do something you may not be very good at, or you may be having an opportunity to finally do something you have always wanted, even though it is no longer in demand. In either case, your company might suffer losses. A more practical approach would see you go through reports and paperwork which would suggest a third alternative, such as investing in real-estate, stocks or elsewhere, to further diversify your company's investment portfolio.

Explore all your options closely and carefully. Do not be limited to a number of options which are apparent. Always remember to seek out better ways to get the same thing done.

Time For The Resolution

All of the four traits and methods we looked into can get you some good information about the issue at hand and the possible resolutions. But, what good is information if nothing can be done from it?

We have gone through the triple A's and learned what started the conflict. We then went on to share what we felt and heard that the other party wasn't exactly feeling all that great either, which is a perfectly natural response towards a conflict.

We then encouraged both parties to share their feelings and share their visions about their plans. Some of the action plans were rather good, while others did not make much sense. Some had ambitious goals but no strategy while others had everything but no definitive goal.

Lastly, we analyzed the situation and then looked for the best solutions possible, including any alternatives out there. Now comes the time to have these shared with the parties and implemented upon.

While both parties are eager to hear what you have to say, it is wise to categorize the information first. This way, both the parties will know exactly what needs to be done.

- Common Goals: This is where you will provide a brief overview of what the common goal is or what exactly seems to be a mutual target. This is something where all the parties would immediately agree. Show them what is evidently and apparently the logical common goal.

- The barriers: Of course, while analyzing the situation, you came across the issues. Provide everyone with an account of what these problems were which initiated the conflict in the first place.

- The finest resolution: Not necessarily the most desired one out there, but it is something to consider. Will each member and party be willing to accept the resolution and live with it? How many would object to it and how many would accept it? You can take further input from all parties and assert that this perhaps might be the best way out of the conflict.

- Compromise is the key: Since we are all looking to resolve matters accordingly, it is only fair that each party gets to compromise a little. If a party or a member is compromising a little too much, it is only fair that they are provided some manner of relief that makes up for the extra compromise. This, of course, is only if there is no better way out. Ideally, a resolution would see all members of parties compromising equally on their stances.

- The big question: Is every party ready to accept the resolution and move forward? Are they all willing to resolve the problem and head towards a better future? If not, you may need to go through the cycle once again.

Conflict resolution isn't exactly a walk in the park. It does take quite a lot of hearing, understanding, analyzing and so much more. There may be times where you may feel like you are circling around and going nowhere. It can get frustrating, but patience is the key. Keep a calm outlook and allow your mind to look past the differences and seek the bigger picture. There is always a resolution that is waiting to come and play its role, and this may very well be the resolution everyone is seeking.

Leaving Room For Improvement

All your efforts to go through the entire ordeal and hear so many variations of the argument have bore some fruit. However, you should always remember that there is a good possibility for a better alternative that may appear much later. You might genuinely feel like you have stumbled upon the best resolution possible, but you never know. All it takes is one variable to change and the entire outcome might be affected.

As a precaution, and perhaps a bit of foresight, keep some flexibility in your resolution. This ensures that your resolution has the tendency of adapting to any new situation that may arise later on after you have implemented said resolution.

Suppose you may be involved in a conflict that revolves around the use of cigarettes within your neighborhood. The issue has increased quite a lot and now threatens the members of the society and the youngsters as well.

Through much deliberation, you have worked out a resolution where both the smokers and the community members have arrived at a mutually agreeable resolution. Both have decided that they will no longer smoke during certain hours, to avoid children being harmed or exposed to this ill habit.

While the resolution makes sense, parties should be prepared to quickly modify and adapt to better strategies. Let's add vaping into the mix. The former smokers now claim that the vapors do not contain any harmful substances and that these are nicotine free. Theoretically, they have a point. To ensure things do not go out of hand, propose a better resolution of discouraging all forms of addictions, including vaping, which can harm adults and children.

Communicate the greater good here while compromising a little yourself. You cannot expect smokers to quit immediately nor can you expect neighbors to impose a thorough ban on smoking. A mutual ground was initially agreed upon but later violated once again, all because of a new variable that was introduced.

Expect plans to change with the passage of time. Do not rule out the possibility of a new conflict nor believe that your resolution will deal with all such conflicts in the future. Leave some room for flexibility and be ready to compromise a little more if you need to. By being stiff, the issue will quickly gain intensity and soon, it will be far beyond your control.

A sign of a successful conflict resolver is that he/she will always leave room for improvement and will always be willing to adapt to the new situation. He/she will never expect a single resolution to be the only solution for almost every conflict of a certain type. Things change every day and so do numerous other variables. To remain on top of your game, be sure to plan well ahead.

Chapter 6:
Conflict In A Digital Age

Back when I was little, things worked quite differently. The world relied more on physical means of communication which normally involved going to a community center or a bar to socialize with people. Everyone would always have time to carry out their routine tasks and still have a laugh or two with their mates on the other side of the city. However, as technology continued to increase, it started to take away quite a lot.

I once predicted that there would come a time where people would be glued to the screens and everything they could ever want would just be a tap away. We're not quite there yet, but we are going there at a rapid pace. Initially, cell phones were introduced to bridge the gap and allow easier communication. Soon, the smartphone came along and now everything we ever need is right within our palm.

It does sound good and convenient, but the elements which have now started to fade, such as exercise and healthy, honest conversations with friends, have started to take a toll on us. There were times where we could go on for ages and be involved in healthy debates and discussions. Now, post a status that says "I support this party" and you will be bombarded with those who don't.

Certainly, we all have a right to an opinion. If I hate football and someone starts making comments about my choices, I would obviously feel slightly disturbed and perhaps a little agitated. This agitation will pretty much eliminate any chance of me ever taking an interest in football, and it is all thanks to this one person who made a completely unnecessary comment.

As the world shifts towards platforms like Facebook, YouTube, Twitter and Reddit, people are growing more and more impatient, and I believe there is a logical reason behind that.

We are living in a day where everyone keeps on sharing the same things over and over again. We develop irrational hatred and false perceptions about things when we come across something so much. Take *Game Of Thrones*, for instance. A friend of mine, who had never even seen a single episode of this TV series, hated the mere mention of GOT. Why? Because everyone on earth was busy singing praises for the show.

We are quick to share everything with the world, thinking that all the likes and comments matter.

If anything, we are probably allowing ourselves to immerse into this fake and virtual world where moral and ethical values are constantly changing. This world is limiting us and our awareness of the actual world, hence causing us to be irritated almost instantly. What makes matters worse is the fact that social media thrives on your irritation. Where you may feel that posting a status is an ideal way to express your disgust or hatred, it is actually inviting conflict to come your way. Social media will further entangle you into tight spots in ways you may have not thought through.

The So-Called Social Media

There are a few things which I firmly believe should remain universal throughout time, and one of them is the way we interact with each other. Social media, while it may have some perks, is far from that. It is a perfect way to start quarrels, chaos, civil unrest and even wars. The top brass of the countries are using social media to spread propaganda while others are using it to mislead the rest of the world. Then there are those who are trying to show the real picture but are subjected to opinions and 'boos' from the general masses. It is a perfect recipe to create a global conflict where even the right opinion is bombarded by sheer negativity.

Considering all that, one begs the question, "How exactly is social media helping us then?" Honestly even I am struggling to figure that out. All I know is that social media certainly contributes in creating hundreds of thousands of conflicts every single day. Make one opinion viral and the world is ready to pour in with their negativity or so-called 'intelligence' to prove the other person wrong.

Taking It Personally

I have a friend who is always tempted to comment on various items on his newsfeed. I have seen some of the posts which he goes through and I have always asked him to refrain from being a party to a conflict. By commenting or proving someone wrong, or even ridiculing their opinion, it automatically triggers a conflict. The funny part is, these two may have never even met each other, and already they hate each other to the core. Why? Just because of a post or a comment he did not accept or agree with? That is absurd, to say the least.

This digital age is indeed entertaining, if you use it the right way, but it is equally devastating as well. The problem isn't in the fact that you may not agree with something. The problem lies in the fact that we have developed this incredibly negative ability to take everything personally.

"Oh, how dare he talk that way about the President?" Frankly, he can. Everyone is entitled to share their opinions. Instead of being upset, learn to accept that there exists an opinion other than yours. Instead of taking things personally, learn how to find the positive aspects. If you cannot find a positive aspect, just ignore it. There is no reason why you should feel compelled to leave a comment and give the person a piece of your mind. That will only make you look dull and daft.

An Unusual Side

We all know that there exists a side within us that rarely gets a chance to manifest itself and speak the bitter truth out and loud. We have learned how to conceal it under the false smiles and laughter, to ensure that we do not end up creating a scene and hurting the general feelings. With the introduction of social media, things have taken a turn for the worse.

Now, we rarely think twice before posting a status, responding to someone's comment or their status, and express our utter displeasure in strong and harsh words. Mind you, we could never muster the courage to do the same in real life, but for some reason we find it easy to do so on social media.

This new side of ours will certainly be raising quite a few eyebrows. Most of these people would be those we rarely ever get to see, let alone meet or interact with. If you stop and think for a moment, you might find it rather odd to involve yourself in a conflict with a person you barely know and may never even meet. Instead, skip past that. Do not let your discrete side come out and tarnish your reputation.

Remember, it is social media we are talking about. All it takes to become the talk of the day is one unusual comment by you; the rest would go viral before you know it.

Vague Content

There are quite a few posts and comments you may come across which may make no sense or which may have some ambiguity and vagueness. I personally recommend avoiding all posts, but then again I do not expect you to do that. Find a middle ground and try to at least identify and mark such posts to rule them out of your newsfeed.

If a specific person or a page posts such content that may be suggestive, hateful or provoking, instead of losing your cool somewhere down the road, it is best to unfollow and remove them from your newsfeed. It literally takes a click and you essentially end any future possibility of a conflict of interest or opinions.

Content That Poses a Threat

While this is rare, I have heard stories about people being bullied and threatened. If you ever encounter such issues, please do not try to resolve such a conflict on your own. Instead, approach the authorities and raise the issue right away.

If someone is trying to harass you or tarnish your reputation through false and misleading statements and posts, approach a lawyer and have it dealt with legally. This way, you are not at the center of the conflict and people who are thorough professionals at resolving conflicts and enforcing law take over to provide you security and safety.

'Mum' Is the Word

There are times you may come across content, posts, or videos which may already be creating quite a buzz. You may already have observed how people are quick to judge you based on a comment regarding such a post. It causes unnecessary friction between people, colleagues, and even family members. What's even worse, if you are feeling low and you decide to post something to share how you feel, people close to you will be the first to pass comments which would further add to the misery.

Since the world is far from being ready to accept each other on social media, it is best to remain quiet and observe. Enjoy the subtle moments instead of being a part of it. Sometimes, the wisest thing to do is to remain far away from issues. It gives you a better perspective and promotes neutrality.

By staying silent and observing, you gain knowledge and analyze things better. There is a reason why the best minds in the world mostly remain quiet and calm while the world continues to create a ruckus for no obvious reason.

Only a person who can remain calm in the face of a difficult time can resolve a conflict productively. Otherwise, the conflict will only be fueled by the additional emotions and aggression you may bring to the table.

Do not react nor comment on what you read. If you like something, just read it on your own. There is no need to share everything you do.

I do see that people now post pictures and 'selfies' literally everywhere they go. They pose with people, with ornaments, with food and so on. Ask them a sensible question or request them to avoid posting and you are immediately met with criticism from the person and his/her peers.

I once asked someone I know to stop posting pictures of every single meal of the day and for once be thankful for what they have. Take a guess what followed. You bet!

If someone is acting abnormally, either distance yourself or be brave enough to comment and then remain calm once the negativity comes knocking at the door. Rest assured, the next time you bump into this person in real life, this person will act completely different. Why? Because now they feel ashamed of facing you and will try to avoid confrontation at any cost.

Other Forms of Digital Communication

Social media is perhaps the biggest part of today's digital age, but it is certainly not the only part in existence. There are other forms of communication which existed well before social media, and they still thrive successfully as they continue to be reliable. However, even these methods come with their unique challenges and can certainly cause conflicts at a moment's notice.

Cell Phones

For our younger readers, you may barely remember this, but there actually was a time when we never had any cell phones on us. We lived perfectly happily and were involved with society on a more personal level. We would write letters and eagerly anticipate a reply, which obviously would take days. We would call our friends on a wired landline only once or twice a week, and we still ended up meeting more than we can imagine today.

Now, with cell phones and smartphones, things have drastically changed. While most would look at the positive aspects, we cannot deny the negative ones either.

Cell phones are becoming a major cause of concern and conflicts for everyone!

It is true. Remember how things would be okay if you failed to answer a call back the same day? Try doing that now and you would be met with the harshest tones possible, demanding an explanation and dictating you never to miss a call ever again.

With applications like WhatsApp, you can read a message and send one in the shortest span of time. The problem arises when you read someone's message and you are in a place where using a cell phone might offend others. Sure, you read and decided to reply later, but this person wouldn't bothered to even consider that you may be busy. Instead, a barrage of messages will follow with angry, red faces and curses. Why? It is absolutely absurd. It is like cell phones have become more of a liability than a tool for better communication.

Every call you get, you are presented with two choices; Accept or Deny. When was the last time you chose the latter, not out of anger, but because you were genuinely busy, and you did not worry of the outcome? Ages ago, maybe!

Conflicts in a digital age are far more frequent than you can imagine. For those who tend to have a quick check on their messages on instant messaging platforms in the middle of the night, they may have faced issues where they were asked to explain why they were "Last seen online" late at night.

I have also had my fair share of conflicts which sprung up between me and my friends. I work with clients where I prefer to keep all distractions away and provide undivided attention to what they have to say. This is a part of my routine, just as it would be with any other person from the same field. However, people still tend to think I am avoiding them deliberately and trying to ignore their calls. While thinking that, they then conjure this feeling of irritation and hatred. Now when I try to speak to them, they would simply not respond properly and further intensify a conflict that began for no valid reason.

Cell phones; yes they are genuinely a good medium to communicate but they are not something we should worship. In every case, we cannot see what the other person is doing when we are calling them. It is only after the other party responds that we are allowed to take a look at their surroundings.

Here are my top two pieces of advice for everyone:

1. Cut down on the excessive use of cell phones. The world will not come crashing down if you stop using your cell phones. It is just an irrational fear that people have developed.

2. Understand that not everyone is in the same situation as you. Having a cell phone does not guarantee you that the other party would always answer your call. Save some room for possibilities.

Chats and Emails

Straight away, I should remind everyone that we cannot see the other party, in most cases. This is why we should try not to start assuming the other person is available or is on the same page as us regarding matters you discuss.

A small example from the world of professionalism

Have you ever wondered why most professionals always use standard fonts and don't type with uppercase letters? Look at the two sentences below and try to see how each of them makes you feel.

- Can you please calm down? There is no need to be so angry.

- CAN YOU PLEASE CALM DOWN? THERE IS NO NEED TO BE SO ANGRY.

I know, most of you figured this out, but to provide everyone with an equal chance of learning, I will explain this.

The first statement seems more like a comforting tone. The second one makes a reader feel like the person is shouting or screaming. While the intention was genuinely to resolve a conflict and allow you to move forward, the uppercase use put a dent on things and changed the entire result altogether.

Whether a professional or a personal email, ensure that you do not use all-caps. It can easily create misunderstandings and can cause quite a lot of issues for you and the other party.

It genuinely helps if we can say the same thing when we are able to see each other. That is only because of our facial expressions and body language. These visible signs are more than enough for anyone to understand the sentiments and emotions, or lack thereof. Take the picture away and you are left with a plain text on the screen, with no reference to the intention or emotion behind the message. Naturally, our mind will assume the worst case scenario first.

I have seen numerous examples by people who believe they are supreme at handling customers and client queries over emails. It only took me about a second to realize the possible outcome of the way they were handling things. Of course, they did not entertain nor approve of my observation. We do have a tendency of taking things personally right away. However, the eventual results were not at all surprising to me, but they did serve as an eye opener for quite a lot of them.

If you are someone who works in an environment where you get to deal with emails and chats, know that your words can drastically change the tone if they are used incorrectly and in the wrong format. You can do a bit of research on this in your free time to learn more. These little tips go a long way to help you become far more effective than you might imagine.

Avoid the obvious trap and start typing using the correct methods. It will genuinely help you become a better communicator, and it is always a benefit to be able to type well anyway.

Nothing Beats Face-To-Face Meetings!

That is a fact, plain and simple. There is absolutely no front where the digital form of communication would shine brighter than the actual communication that takes place in real-life meetings between people.

To begin with, there is no ambiguity. Everyone can see and feel everything. There is no misunderstanding, as anything said can easily be repeated, rephrased, and explained. You can immediately apologize for anything that you may have said wrong, and everyone will easily figure out by your body language that you genuinely mean it.

Communication involves quite a lot of non-verbal elements in order to be truly perfect. While the digital age has its complications, there are virtually none when it comes to the physical, person to person meeting in real life at a physical venue. I know, some of you may have thought that video calls can help eliminate doubts, but frankly it does not help.

Anyone can fake a smile or act as if everything is fine on a video call. Plus, the image quality further helps to hide hints which otherwise would be evident. There are no "weak signals" to worry about and any issue that may arise can be dealt with easily.

So why am I talking about real-life meetings then if it has everything to do with ways to avoid conflict but none to resolve one? Simple!

It is understood that in most of the conflicts that emerge with family or friends, we would first try to learn more about it through a phone call or a video call. It is indeed a good start, but not the ideal one. Pretty soon, you might find that you cannot get the information you need and that you are going around in circles. When you truly need to resolve the issues, ask the parties to meet in real life.

The real-life will take away any ambiguity or vagueness in communication. Now, the parties would be there, facing each other. With a calm mind, approach the matter and start resolving issues maturely. There is a reason why most corporate giants prefer to resolve conflicts in real-life meetings over doing so using digital means. It produces far better results and allows everyone to know what exactly is going on.

The Digital Bullies

I kid you not, they do exist. They are very real and can often be found messing with other people's lives for no obvious reasons. Whether you are someone who is seeking an answer at a reputable platform or sharing your achievements with the world on a page, they will find their way to you and try to harass you.

Bullies, digital or otherwise, are unwanted. They can easily mess up the entire situation and turn the rather joyful moment into an embarrassing situation. While most of these bullies might only be looking to crash the party, or the post in this case, they may not necessarily pose any threat or harm. It is easy to avoid them by blocking them, and that would be the end of it.

Other ways to avoid would be to provide a logical response that is neither offensive nor irrelevant or provoking in any way. If the bully has any sense, the comments and party crashing should stop almost immediately.

In some rare cases, there are those who have reported being threatened by bullies. Whether for money or other worldly gains, this is unethical and falls under the jurisdiction of cybercrime and cyber-harassment. If you or anyone you know of experiences this, approach the concerned authorities right away. Try not to take matters into your own hands.

These threats can be received in quite a few ways. More recently, people have reported that a group of hackers managed to enter their system through some dummy link and encrypt all the files. To unlock it, they demand a hefty payment. Even after a few paid up, the files were never recovered and the hackers still managed to walk away with the money. The worst thing is, there is no way to communicate with these groups of cyber bullies, and therefore there is no possible way to find a resolution. The best that can be suggested is to backup your important data and keep it safe in a separate drive for maximum security.

For almost every other kind of cyber bully, you have quite a few ways to tackle them. If needed, you can even get in touch with a few to find out just why they are causing such a nuisance. There is a chance you might actually be able to engage in a healthy conversation where the person might share the details about the issues he/she may have with a post or a person.

If such cases arrive, be sure to understand and respect their points of view and opinions. You can then share your side of the issues, such as how their comments or bullying affect the general audience and you. You can try to negotiate and arrive at a point where the person will stop bullying and others can stop doing things to trigger a call for revenge. A win-win for everyone at any given day.

Lastly, it is also advisable to refrain from acting like a bully yourself. A common belief exists that bullies get more fame and fortune owing to their confidence to deal with issues and take charge of matters. If that was the case, some of the top names in this world would have comprised of a large number of people who would have been bullies. Is that the case? Not at all!

Chapter 7:
Know When It's Time To Walk Away

Finally, we have covered almost all the essential phases, seen quite a few examples, learned about some tips and tricks, and have started changing the way we look at things. While all that goes on, there is still a gaping hole that is yet to be filled. There is still something that seems amiss.

Rest assured that there will be conflicts where you will try your best effort, and you will do everything by the book, yet the results will be anything but forthcoming. You will remain calm, you will remain composed, you will follow all the necessary steps and use all the relevant tools to analyze the problem and come to a logical resolution that is acceptable by all members. Needless to say, you will still end up feeling as if you are banging your head against a wall that is far from even budging an inch, let alone moving.

When such situations strike, what do you expect we do? Should we cower and hide from the seemingly uncontrollable conflict or should we continue to push on, hoping against hope that we get a breakthrough? Surprisingly, in such cases, it is best to call it a day and just take a step back; you read it correct, walk away!

If there was a way that our intentions could change the outcome of the conflict, we would perhaps be leading a very different life. Unfortunately, our intentions are mostly far from being visible or in any way impactful. We, therefore, need to take some action to actually acquire the results we want.

There are numerous conflicts which take place within a family almost every other day. This is quite normal. What is not normal is how we deal with conflicts. Most of us start the conflict or are made a party midway and then blamed for almost everything that went wrong. While people hurl words, and at times objects, at us, we are left to wonder how on earth can we restore sanity and control the situation. Let me be the first one to tell you, if it is silly or repetitive, walk away.

There are people who seek to resolve conflicts or avoid them, and then there are people who cause them deliberately, just to get some fun out of witnessing others fight. I know of a person who happens to be a brother of my friend, and straight away I can tell that he seeks out ways to cause chaos and create conflicts between family members. Why? Simply because that's how he is.

We come across such a person in almost every family on earth. There is this person who is always looking to create trouble for others. It is okay to explain to them once, twice or even three times, but explaining the same thing over and over again, and clearing up the conflict he/she may have created can be redundant and pointless.

By continuing your support for such a person, you are theoretically encouraging this type of behavior. You are letting this person know that you will always be there to cover up for any mess that may be caused in the wake of a conflict. What you should be doing instead is letting them know they are on their own. Walk away from the conflicts and dispel any connection. Let them know they should now deal with matters on their own and that you will have nothing to do with any of the issues related to him/her.

There will be two interesting results from this:

1. This person will now cease all such activities since his/her backup (i.e. you) just walked away.

2. The conflict will immediately lose most of its intensity, allowing for peaceful talks to finally be a viable option.

I do admit that walking away from a conflict is easier said than done. To begin with, you get the feeling as if you are quitting or giving up. Then, there is your ego that constantly pushes you to get back into the conflict and have another go. Controlling all these aspects is quite a bit of a challenge, one that requires a mammoth amount of tolerance, acceptance and patience.

Here's my suggestion for anyone who may wish to try walking away from a conflict; think of the bigger picture at stake. If you, by walking away, will end up diffusing the situation and avoid a certain argument and an unnecessary fight, it is best to take the higher ground and take a step back. Let the dust settle and then analyze the situation calmly. Emotions, when they run high, can often force us to make some radical decisions, and it goes without saying that these decisions often lead to disastrous consequences.

I would like to stress that not all conflicts should result in a walk away. Therefore, it is time to learn more about ways to identify and know when the time is right to call it quits.

The Part Where You Walk Away

Let us begin by discussing an example. In this example we will be observing a couple who argue over matters almost every day.

The husband is generally a person who is quite laid back and works flexible hours. The wife, on the other hand, has weekend classes to attend apart from taking care of the house, the kitchen, and two kids. Naturally, the wife would feel stressed out and might vent out the frustration of constantly working without a break.

Arguments come and go between the two, and almost every time, the wife would complain that the husband is not doing much. The husband would respond with counter-arguments which are generally overlooked or unappreciated. This obviously causes quite a bit of friction between the two and the long, never-ending conflict carries on and on, and on.

In such a case, if any of the two would just walk away from an argument, the conflict would immediately change directions and lose intensity. Care should be taken though; walk away without informing or rudely and you just might be inviting yet another conflict your way.

In such a similar case, if one party is complaining and not ready to hear your side of the story, walking away is perhaps a fine option. This is not a personal opinion but a professional one. The reason is rather simple.

In order to resolve any conflict, you will need to hear the party and respect their opinion, and be heard and respected as well. Then, both parties will need to compromise fairly and equally to arrive at mutually agreeable ground. Since here, one party is refusing to hear what the other party has to say, the rest will never take place. Instead of yelling or losing your temper, apologize and walk away.

I guarantee you one thing, you will have this burning sensation within your chest region and you will be tempted to respond or yell or scream back something rude that you may feel like the party deserves. I also guarantee that if you do this and respond, you will now become a new reason for a prolonged conflict. Remain calm and simply let time do its magic.

It may take some time and the mood may remain a bit gloomy and dull, but eventually, sense will prevail and the other party will be ready to discuss matters with you maturely.

Walk Away And Get Help

There may be conflicts which would begin as usual but end up with some severe results. I am of course referring to the ones where one party or person may end up threatening others.

Sure enough, it is always advisable to walk away from such instances, but sometimes, walking away isn't the only thing you should do. You should seek assistance first since your life or physical well-being may be threatened here.

Involving the local authorities is a smart first step to ensure your safety and the safety of those you hold dear. What matters most here is to ensure you walk away secretly or nicely, whichever is applicable. Once done, let the local authorities know how you have been threatened and leave the rest to them.

Sometimes, these threats come from people we love, and that is a very heart-breaking and gut-wrenching moment. We never expect someone we hold dear to be able to threaten us, and when it happens, it will most certainly tarnish the reputation of the person permanently.

You might be tempted, out of compassion and love, to talk things through with the person and make them see some sense, but it shouldn't take you long to realize when to back off. The minute abuses are being hurled, threats are sent out or you are being provoked, walk away instead of responding to any of these. If the threat is serious, involve the authorities and worry about the relation later.

Keep your safety the number one priority; whatever happens afterwards can be dealt with as long as you are safe.

I Shall Not Compromise

So be it! There is no point in trying to convince someone to drop the theatrics and resolve the conflict if said person is anything but sensible. By now, it should be something that everyone knows; in order to resolve a conflict, there must be a mutual consensus, and that consensus requires some compromise from both sides.

If one party bluntly refuses to budge an inch, stop right there. You can push a wall for as long as you like, the only thing that will fall is you. Stubbornness will always get in the way of a healthy discussion, debate or argument. It can ruin moods, destroy relationships and cause issues of the highest order. Controlling this element might be easy if it is a part of our personality, but controlling someone else's stubborn attitude is no piece of cake. Even experts at times throw in the towel when trying to break through the stubbornness of people.

Make it a general rule in life: if the other person is ready to compromise and respect your position, proceed to resolving the conflict. Anything else and it's best to walk away.

No Sign of Hope

We have all been there and have witnessed this happening to quite a lot of people, including our friends, members of the family and within our offices as well. A person starts ranting on and continuously blames the other. Despite everyone trying to calm the situation, this person is not showing signs of stopping or calming down.

The longer you stay in such a conflict, the more the chances of this person completely losing their temper. As a sign of respect for yourself and for others, get up and walk away.

Resolving a conflict when even one of the sides is acting in such a manner is never a possible outcome. You will end up being hurled with abuses, and possibly physical harm as well. While you walk away, it should allow everyone to get a grip on their emotions and calm down. The next round can begin whenever everyone feels ready.

Here's a twist though: what if it is your boss who is losing their temper for all the wrong reasons, and you really can't stand it anymore? As hard as this may sound, apologize and let your boss know you will be ready to explain once he is ready to hear you out. Stand up and walk out. Do not say anything that might further fuel the fire.

Now, I do understand some may end up losing their jobs, but if you are certain you were being blamed for no obvious reason and without proof, you can always search for a better job and in the meantime file a lawsuit against your former boss. I'm not saying that this is something you should do, but it is always an option that you can resort to when things get a little too out of hand.

The reason it is okay to leave such a boss is simple; if they cannot handle their anger issues, it is very easy for them to lose their patience at odd times and that may spell trouble for quite a lot of employees, who will then be needed to cover the mess up. I, personally, would never recommend anyone put up with such issues. You are a human being, a free soul, not a slave. Find a better job, and as soon as you get one, quit this one. The longer you remain in such a firm, the more stressed out you will start to be. The more stress, the less you will be able to focus on matters which really matter.

When You Are Being Shut Down

"No, you listen to me…"

"I don't care what you think…"

"Do you think I care about what you have to say?"

If a conflict, argument, or debate has any of this going on, it is a strong indicator that you should walk away without wasting any more of your valuable time.

Everyone deserves respect, and everyone has a right to speak and to be heard. If someone is trying to reign supreme and completely shut you out, whether out of annoyance, anger, status or any other reason, you are wasting your time and putting your integrity on the line just by being there. There is no reason for you to stay a second longer and be a party to a one-sided affair where whatever you say or do does not matter at all.

Walk away and let things settle on their own. Walking away is one of the strongest ways to get back at someone. It is also a sound indicator for anyone with a remote sense of moral values. As soon as they calm down, they will realize they went over the line and thus should seek ways to apologize and make things better.

Of course, there are cases where they will not be the least bothered and may not even come back to have a word with you, and I am not including your boss or supervisor. I am, in fact, referring to instances at home and with friends.

We all break into arguments and there is not a single couple out there that can claim that they have never argued before. Therefore, it is perfectly normal if you find yourself arguing almost every other day. The part that you should worry about is how you handle these arguments and conflicts. Whether it is selecting a new piece of furniture or trying to decide whom to invite for the Thanksgiving turkey dinner, handle things by hearing both sides of the story and then coming to a logical conclusion.

Try not to overlook your partner's viewpoint or wishes. If one of you is being a little too selfish and making decisions without considering the other, you are heading towards a path that may see you eventually divided into two egos at war, and that is never good news.

Slam The Door Or Leave Quietly?

You probably have wondered at times how to exit the stage without adding any more to the drama and theatrics. You may have felt like you are just going to make matters worse by being there for longer durations and hence decide to get up and walk away. You are being constantly victimized and abused by the other person as you walk away. Just as you reach the door, they throw something at you, and something within you snaps! What follows are fists and kicks, swinging to connect to a jaw or a cheek. It will end up with broken bones, bloodied noses and possibly handcuffs as someone takes the two of you for a ride to the local police station.

I am not surprised by the fact that most of us have no idea how to walk away from conflicts. We know what we want before a conflict begins. We know what we need to say during a conflict, and we even know how walking away will resolve most of the issues, but we have never pondered over how we will actually do that.

There are those who decide to walk away and while doing so end up throwing something towards the other; not good! There are those who will walk to the door and say "You know what, F*** you!" Really? What's the point in walking away if you cannot control your emotions?

The entire exercise of walking away is to allow you to remain in control of your emotions and not let them take control of your actions and thinking. By walking away, you are saving yourself quite a lot of trouble and keeping your dignity and respect. You are also damaging the other party's ego in a way, which for some has a subtle sense of victory. Whatever tickles your fancy, walk away when you see any of the hints above mentioned.

It is time to look at possible exit strategies and how to use them so that you are well prepared to handle one-sided conflicts.

Listen, Listen, Listen!

One thing we do tend to skip is the part where we sit down and listen to the other person. Remember active listening? This is pretty much the same thing. The only difference here is that the other party is yelling or disregarding your opinions and continually trying to force you into submission.

All the loud talking, all the harsh words and all the resentful comments, all of them are thrown at you, but instead of using empathy or nodding your head, stay silent. Be patient and wait for the other person to vent out as much as they can or as much as you can endure. Once one of the elements ends, stand up and excuse yourself out of the room.

"Well, if that is it, then I shall be heading outside. I hope for the best for you and everyone else."

That alone should hit the bullseye. Remember, the objective here is not to agitate the other party further, but to walk out of a messy situation with grace.

"Wait, if grace is all that mattered, I could have done that without the 'listening' part."

While that is true, you would have missed out on one important point; learning. Conflicts are either seen as threats or opportunities. You can either fight or flight, the two most common and natural responses of a human being to any conflict. The world continues to live with a mindset that winning conflicts makes one superior. That is absurd and completely wrong.

Instead, think of conflicts this way; when they come, you get an opportunity to observe someone a little more closely, especially the part that is normally away from sight. You get to see how the other party reacts, how they may try to handle their emotions and how good or otherwise they are when it comes to resolving conflicts. Learning all this is crucial as it changes your perception about them and gives you a good understanding of whether or not the other party can be trusted.

If you are in a conflict, you should force yourself to learn and forget worrying about who will win or lose the conflict. They may walk away with a sense of victory but you will be walking away with knowledge and experience that will help you resolve or avoid so much more in life and make you a better person. This is only possible if you can muster enough endurance to listen and pay attention to what is being said.

Be Concise

One of the toughest obstacles we face as human beings is keeping ourselves in check during a potentially heated argument or conflict. We easily fall for the obvious trap and lose our sight and sense of objective which leads us to state things we either did not mean or could have put in better words. Either way, it is a catastrophe that was waiting to happen.

If you are looking for an easier way to keep calm and remain to the point, and ensure all possible chances of an all-out war of words are kept at bay, I am sorry to disappoint but there is no greater way than practice.

Some of the finest conflict resolvers, professional or otherwise, are known for knowing how to choose their words carefully and state only what is needed, free of any emotions. The minute you let your emotions tamper with your feelings and sentiments, you will most likely end up with the following result:

Objective: "I highly doubt this would work. I believe it is best for us all to try finding another way."

What we end up saying instead: "You've got to be joking. Even my grandma can do this better than you. You know what, you rest your highness, let someone with a bit more brains think of something!"

Harmful, insulting, absolutely unneeded and above all, not the need of the hour. While the idea has somewhat remained the same, the delivery was far from being acceptable. Using such tones is like standing in front of a speeding train. You know it will not stop in time and there is every possibility of it ending up crushing you.

Your words should reflect only what you intend to talk about in the conflict. Remain determined and calm. Your statements should be clear and concise, with no room left for questions or comments. The more concise they are, the sooner you can walk away.

If you were in a conflict trying to let your colleague know that you do not support their recent move, don't just yell out things. Try this:

"I have heard what you had to say. I only wanted to ensure that your move will not land us in hot water. I do not intend that you follow my way, I just wanted to ensure you follow the right way. I believe it would be appropriate to call it a day for now. Both of us could use a little time to ponder over what to do next."

Respectful and at the same time as clear as crystal. You have shown your concern for the person and the outcome that the conflict is leading towards. You have shown that you do not support their view nor are trying to impose your ideas either. Then, you have called it a day to allow yourself and the other person to have some personal space.

The Obvious

In all of the situations above, the eventual result will see us "Get up and leave" and that is precisely what we should do.

When I say get up and leave, I honestly mean to get up and leave, and do nothing else in between. This is the hardest part of the entire conflict. The minute you get up to leave, after having informed the other person of your departure, we get this massive urge to shout something, pass a comment or do anything to offend the other party. Trust me, that is a recipe for disaster.

Do not give into the temptation and focus on leaving the general area quietly. Let the conflict be limited to that specific zone only. Do not leave the room with the intention of bad mouthing or sharing all the details with others waiting outside. The more you share, the more public the issue becomes, and the more people know about this conflict, the easier it will be for things to get out of hand.

There is no science behind how you should get up and leave, therefore, stick to the basics. On your way out, in case you are in a closed room, ensure to close the door gently as you would normally do. Do not slam the door or shut it loudly to show your frustration. There is no need for that as that is simply immature and unprofessional.

Wait for a reaction

Whether you have already walked away from a conflict, or you are planning to walk away, it might help to actually wait it out a little. Sometimes, waiting allows us to get some kind of reaction which then serves us with some information and an idea about how we can proceed ahead.

While you may not need to wait long, in some cases, keep in mind that there is a higher chance you may have to wait and kill your anxiousness for a while before you get any kind of reaction from the other party. The reasons behind the delays depend upon how soon the other party cools off and starts thinking rationally.

It is also to be observed that conflict resolution is a two-way street. That means that you too should use the time and think matters through clearly. There should be no ambiguity and you should take every step to see if you were at fault. If so, be ready to apologize the next time you speak. If not, be sure to ask the right questions and suggest a positive way out of the conflict which would benefit both of you.

Wherever waiting is involved, anxiousness and curiosity will find their way. There are times when you may end up arguing with your friend over some conflicting matter and walk away from the situation. That is where you find yourself unable to wait for a return text message or call. You will be tempted to pick up the phone and get in touch with the person.

You may use made-up stories or just call and say you mistakenly dialed their number; we all know this does not work. Instead, if you are unable to wait that long, let them know that you are willing to look past this incident and that you are hoping to get things back to normal and be more vigilant to ensure conflicts like these do not repeat again. This way, they feel happy, you get your friend back and both of you try to make things better for each other.

Some Last Minute Tips

Here are a few more tips for you to remember and implement whenever you face a tough conflict. These are applicable both in personal and professional settings, and should allow you to get the desired results:

- **Resolution for two** - Remain focused on the task at hand. Every conflict takes place to achieve something. If you know what you want to achieve, remain focused on it. Do not deviate from your goal and use words and suggestions that further highlight how the resolution you seek would benefit all members. Look at the broader picture and see what fits best for all while forgetting your personal inclination and wishes.

- **Hang in there** - Serious talks, loud voices, sobs and cries, all are part of conflicts. Do not let emotions get the best of you and remain steadfast. You are a part of the conflict and you intend to make things right for yourself and for everyone you care about. Hang in there!

- **Right to feel this way -** If you feel let down on some action, it is very much a possibility that the other person may have felt the same about something you did. Respect each other's position and know that each of you have the right to feel this way and act the way you are. Do not look upon someone's behavior and jump to conclusions without assessing the cause behind it.

- **Say no to judgments and blame games -** The worst part about any conflict is how people are quick to judge a person and shift the blame on them. There is no point in blaming each other, nor is there any reason for you to be judgmental just because you cannot see eye to eye. Try and find the real reason why things aren't working the way you would like them to. It is possible that both parties may not be at fault and that an external issue is what made the entire conflict emerge.

- **Speaking nothing more than the truth -** The minute you start to add even a single word of lie, you are corrupting the result of the conflict. Stay with the truth, even if it means to admit your own mistakes. Trust me, it is better to do that instead of lie and then be caught by someone else.

- **Lose them, not yourself** - This is the toughest part in relationships where a person you care about is involved. You have a choice, either to lose yourself and become someone you are not, or to lose that person and keep your integrity. If the issues are continuous, take a deep breath and take the step to walk away for good. Do not lose yourself or your personal integrity by doing something you will regret for the rest of your life.

- **If they can't get back to their senses, there's no need to chase** - Well, you had a terrible fight and things went out of hand rather quickly. You were trying your best to make things right but ended up being a victim to countless comments, abuses and possibly even a punch or two. You remained calm and eventually walked away. The clock has started and you have decided to wait for the other party to snap back into their senses. While this does seem ideal, you should know that there are limits to almost everything. You cannot put your life on hold just so someone can come to their senses and apologize. If they are too stubborn and naive to realize your worth, let them go. There is no point in hoping for a lost cause to return back, especially if they never attempted to have a word with you directly. Take the higher road and cut them away from your life for good.

With all of the knowledge, tips, and tricks, you are now ready to take a life-altering step forward and become a better person for yourself, personally and professionally. You have seen it all, and now you know how to conquer all.

Yes, I do not expect that you will be resolving all the conflicts, every single time, but what I do expect is that you will take each of the conflicts as an opportunity to learn more and find better resolutions for yourself and other parties.

Through conflict resolution, you will be resolving conflicts at home, within your neighborhood, workplace and even within the community. People will look up to you and that will solely be to seek your help and assistance to have their issues resolved.

It takes practice, and I mean a lot of practice, in order to gain a competitive edge and learn how to handle even the toughest conflicts without worries. Now go on out there, and show the world that you have what it takes to resolve conflicts.

Conclusion

Conflicts - a word that instills a sense of fear, poses a threat, and to some it poses as a challenging opportunity. Look at it anyway you please, and in all ways, you will find it to be a challenge.

They arrive when you least expect them, and they can turn a simple difference of opinion into an outrage for one and a ridiculous idea for another. We already know how simple conflicts play out, but what we least ponder upon is how we will proceed to resolve said conflicts. That is where conflict resolution comes into play.

Conflict resolution is a skill, a method and a way through which we find a peaceful and a mutually-agreeable solution to a conflict. This could be as simple as apologizing to something as significant as signing peace treaties to end decades old conflict between regions.

Since conflicts are natural, it is only fair to say that conflict resolution holds a very significant place in the lives of everyone. Whether you are a professional who gets to deal with hundreds of employees every day, or a parent who gets to resolve conflicts between offspring, you need to know what you are doing. Without knowledge and control of your emotions, you will end up creating a bigger mess than you can manage.

Throughout the book, we learned various techniques and went through a handful of examples. All of them provided an in-depth look into how you can successfully resolve conflicts.

Right at the beginning, I mentioned that this book would serve you with some of the most powerful methods, tips and tricks which you should know of and have within your toolbox. I am glad to report that I have provided all there is to know and learn to handle life's most challenging situations.

Yes, there are instances where I have advised you to avoid or even walk away. While that may sound strange, it is only to diminish the tension within the air. The more stressed you are, the more room there is for an error in judgement. It is perfectly okay to know and accept that you are not able to handle a situation at a given time. We are human beings after all; you cannot expect to win every time nor handle all conflicts perfectly.

A Quick Recap

Before our journey could even begin, there was a matter that needed addressing. Many, if not all, look at conflicts as unusual and unwanted events in life. I do agree with the latter as it is genuinely bad in most cases, but I do beg to differ on the former part. It is not at all unusual, and that is what everyone needs to know and realize first.

Start by changing your mind about conflicts and accept them as natural occurrences. They happen between the best couples, best friends and even the finest employees and the kindest employers on earth.

We started our journey with perhaps the most important skill of the lot, and that is **active listening**. Simply put, it is a method through which you get to know more about what is bothering the other party. Using traits like empathy, listening patiently and intently allows you to dig in deeper and make the other person know and feel that you care. This allows easier flow of information and room for any ambiguity is brought down to a fraction, if not completely shut off.

By paying close attention and using some friendly, reassuring words, the other party should easily be able to share with you some details which could possibly provide you with a solution that is acceptable to both sides.

As a conflict resolution expert, it is your job to take responsibility for your own actions and let others know it is okay to make a mistake at the same time. You can do that by apologizing for any mistake that you may have made which might have fueled the conflict to this stage. The minute you do so, you are letting them know that you are happy to help make things better. You are also promoting a sense of relief for the other party by lowering your ego. This, as a result, will ensure they do the same. What is then left is just healthy discussion and possibly a feasible solution for both.

Active listening plays a great role in cases where you are unable to see the party and are nowhere near each other. This usually happens when you are trying to resolve conflicts over emails, phone calls, or texts. Remain calm and composed. Use words which show your intention to accept mistakes and look past mistakes made by the other party. Let them know that you are ready to look at the bigger picture that would serve in the best interest for both.

Conflicts are not always bad either. There are times where you may enter into conflicts and then decide to speak truth and remain honest. Yes, being honest and speaking the truth may not be cheered by many, but it is best for everyone to speak the truth and leave no room for vagueness or doubts.

We also saw how we should never take conflicts

as personal attacks. That is because as soon as we look upon conflicts as attacks by the other party members, we will immediately stop looking for a solution and start thinking of a counter-attack option. This then will be a never-ending vicious cycle of attack after attack; when the conflict will end is anybody's guess. Without active listening, most of what followed within the book is not fully possible.

We then started learning about some of the most powerful techniques which included:

- Being neutral and non-judgmental

- Knowing and respecting the other perspective

- Knowing that you can be wrong

- Effective communication

- Honesty

- Emotional intelligence

- Patience

- Impartiality

The list goes on and on. It soon dawned upon us that conflicts do not necessarily happen between family members or workplace colleagues only; there are instances where conflicts may emerge over in the digital world, too.

We went into the depths of social media and looked at how easily it can spread a simple conflict like wildfire where all opinions, right or wrong, are judged and discouraged by the very same people who talk about fairness and rights. We saw how difficult things can get in today's digital age, but fortunately we also learned how we can improve our digital communication to handle such issues.

Yes, there were instances where I mentioned you can completely eradicate the chances of facing a conflict, but for that, you need to know what your response would sound like. Should you be using uppercase letters or lowercase letters to type in your next email? Would that make any difference? Certainly.

The book eventually provided details on a rather odd-sounding trait, and that is to know when to walk away from a fight.

Fight or flight, a natural human response to any situations that may pose stress or threat. Those who fight would use anything and everything for their defense while those who 'flight' would be laughed at for being cowards, right? Wrong! Sometimes, exiting the stage is exactly what the situation calls for. Conflicts are not meant to be won or lost, they are meant to improve on the situation and end in a solution that will help everyone in general. However, if one party is refusing to cooperate or lower their ego, it is best to walk away and put a little distance between yourself and the other party.

Use the time to think things through and when the contact is established again, clear the air with honesty. Whether you both arrive at a logical conclusion or not depends on how both parties handle the issue.

Through mature and sensible practices, conflicts can be resolved. By rushing into being judgmental or assuming things, you are only putting a dent on your chances of successfully resolving a conflict.

Practice Is The Key

I could not have put it better - Without practice, you can never be a good problem solver, let alone a master of conflict resolution. The more you practice with the skills and tips shared within this book, the easier things will become for you.

I do not mean that you should practice by deliberately creating a scene and then trying things out to resolve conflicts. Instead, note these down within a diary or a notepad. Use these when situations call for it, and remember never to cave in unless you are sure you made a mistake.

Remain honest and truthful about everything. The rewards would justify your efforts to remain crystal clear.

There are hundreds of videos and tutorials out there, each teaching a unique trick or two. However, almost all of those videos will ask you to follow the same basic steps and build on the same skills shared within this book. That is simply because these tricks, tips, or methods are universally accepted as helpful.

Conflict resolution is tough, I will not lie. It will get tougher as you practice, I will not say it won't either. With that said though, I will certainly say this; once you develop tolerance and learn how to control your emotions, you will see a significant change within yourself and your ability to solve issues.

There have been no greater conflicts than the two world wars we have read within the history books. Each of them started with conflicts and eventually ended with table talks. These table talks were led by experts who knew how to resolve conflicts just like you and me. Back in the day, with little knowledge, they were able to do something so historic.

Fortunately, we now have quite a lot of knowledge available within seconds. If they were able to pull off such a remarkable feat with limited knowledge, imagine where you can go with so much more knowledge. All you need is a mind that is ready to do the best and prepared to expect the worst.

Mastering all of these will make you into a role model for many to learn from and follow. This also means that people will be looking up to you to resolve quite a lot of conflicts which they simply cannot manage or withstand. Take it from a person who has experienced this first hand that people will truly seek your advice and work on whatever you have to say.

It is a great responsibility as well, but instead of worrying too much about it, consider the reward of feeling great about yourself and knowing that your advice was able to change someone's life in one way or the other. Your words will no longer be mere words as they will now hold a certain charm and wisdom. Lead by example and lead confidently.

Occasionally, you might want to take a break, which is perfectly fine. The more relaxed and energized you are, the merrier the results will be for you and everyone around you.

Finally, it is time for us to part ways. I do certainly hope that you have found a way or two to help you resolve most of the conflicts within life. I cannot tell you enough how important practice and patience are. Practice as much as you can and, as a bonus tip, learn how to meditate as well.

With a combination of meditation, stress relieving techniques, and conflict resolution skills, you will be resolving situations without ever finding yourself in a spot of trouble. With that, I wish you the best of luck in resolving your next big conflict with style and finesse. Be confident and be ready, because now you know everything there is to conflict resolution.

References

Carroll, M. (2012, January). Resolving Conflict by Exploring Different Perspectives. Retrieved January 12, 2020, from https://www.nlpacademy.co.uk/articles/view/resolving_conflict_by_exploring_different_perspectives/

Manson, M. (2019, October 29). 5 Skills to Help You Develop Emotional Intelligence. Retrieved January 11, 2020, from https://markmanson.net/emotional-intelligence

Miller, C. (1970, January 3). On Meditation and Leadership. Retrieved January 18, 2020, from http://sixandahalfconsulting.com/blog/5-ways-manage-conflict/

Paul, M. (2014, March 23). Conflict: 7 Decisions to Learn Instead of Fight. Retrieved January 21, 2020, from https://www.huffpost.com/entry/conflict-resolution_b_4632104

Shonk, K. (2019, October 14). What is Conflict Resolution, and How Does It Work? Retrieved January 5, 2020, from https://www.pon.harvard.edu/daily/conflict-resolution/what-is-conflict-resolution-and-how-does-it-work/

Wolf, R., & Nagy, J. (n.d.). Section 6. Training for Conflict Resolution. Retrieved January 20, 2020, from https://ctb.ku.edu/en/table-of-contents/implement/provide-information-enhance-skills/conflict-resolution/main